Test of Adult Basic Education Study Guide:

TABE Test Prep and Practice Test Questions

Free From Stress to Success DVD from Trivium Test Prep

Dear Customer,

Thank you for purchasing from Trivium Test Prep! Whether you're looking to join the military, get into college, or advance your career, we're honored to be a part of your journey.

To show our appreciation (and to help you relieve a little of that test-prep stress), we're offering a **FREE *From Stress to Success* DVD** by Trivium Test Prep. Our DVD includes 35 test preparation strategies that will help keep you calm and collected before and during your big exam. All we ask is that you email us your feedback and describe your experience with our product. Amazing, awful, or just so-so: we want to hear what you have to say!

To receive your **FREE *From Stress to Success* DVD**, please email us at 5star@triviumtestprep.com. Include "Free 5 Star" in the subject line and the following information in your email:

1.   The title of the product you purchased.

2.   Your rating from 1 – 5 (with 5 being the best).

3.   Your feedback about the product, including how our materials helped you meet your goals and ways in which we can improve our products.

4.   Your full name and shipping address so we can send your **FREE *From Stress to Success* DVD**.

If you have any questions or concerns please feel free to contact me directly.

Thank you, and good luck with your studies!

Alyssa Wagoner

Quality Control

alyssa.wagoner@triviumtestprep.com

Table of Contents

Table of Contents

Introduction

The fact that you've purchased this book means two things. The first is that you're preparing for, or at least considering taking, the TABE exam, which can open new doors for your future by greatly expanding your options for careers. The second is that you've already taken an excellent first step in picking up this study guide.

We'll provide you with a detailed overview of the TABE, so that you know exactly what to expect on test day, then we'll cover all of the subjects over which you will be tested, providing multiple practice sections for you to test your knowledge and improve. Even if it's been a while since your last major examination, don't worry; we'll make sure you're more than ready!

What is the TABE?

The TABE exam measures your skills through the high school level in Language Arts, Reading, and Mathematics. In short, it tests everything taught in high school, so employers and institutions will know that you are prepared for new training.

Breaking Down the TABE

Reading
- 50 questions, 50 minute time limit. Tests ability to read and interpret written passages.

Mathematics
- There are 2 separate math sections on the TABE, however, for purposes of studying we will cover it in one chapter. While the presentation of questions is slightly different in each section, it really does not matter how the question is posed if you understand the fundamentals of math. It always comes down to adding, subtracting, multiplying, and dividing.
  - Math Comprehension: 40 questions, 25 minute time limit.
  - Math Application: 50 questions, 50 minute time limit.

Language, Language Mechanics, Vocabulary, Spelling
- Tests knowledge of sentence structure, usage, mechanics, grammar, and organization. For purposes of this study guide, all sections are taught together. As you know, language, spelling, and vocabulary are all connected. Only the Language section is required; Language Mechanics, Vocabulary, and Spelling are optional.
  - Language: 55 questions, 55 minute time limit.
  - Language Mechanics (optional section): 20 questions, 14 minute time limit
  - Vocabulary (optional section): 20 questions, 15 minute time limit.
  - Spelling (optional section): 20 questions, 10 minute time limit.

Scoring

There is no set passing or failing score on the TABE. You will need to check with the school or employment agency to find out what their minimum standards are. The scoring criteria is rather complicated, requiring a few different charts for each section. For many people, if you can get 70% of more of the question correct while working through this book, you should do fine.

How This Book Works

The subsequent chapters in this book are divided into a review of those topics covered on the exam. This is not to "teach" or "re-teach" you these concepts – there is no way to cram all of that material into one book! Instead, we are going to help you recall all of the information that you've already learned. Even more importantly, we'll show you how to apply that knowledge.

Each chapter includes an extensive review, with practice drills at the end to test your knowledge. With time, practice, and determination, you'll be completely prepared for test day.

Chapter 1: The Reading Section

The Reading portion of the TABE will measure your ability to evaluate, analyze, and understand written passages. Tested passages will contain material from a variety of sources and on a number of different topics; after reading those passages, you will then have 50 minutes within which to answer 50 multiple-choice questions. Remember that the information in this section is applicable for other sections of the test! Reading, vocabulary, grammar, and spelling are all tied together in the English Language.

The Main Idea

The main idea of a text is the purpose behind why a writer would choose to write a book, article, story, etc. Being able to find and understand the main idea is a critical skill necessary to comprehend and appreciate what you're reading.

Consider a political election. A candidate is running for office and plans to deliver a speech asserting her position on tax reform. The **topic** of the speech—tax reform—is clear to voters, and probably of interest to many. However, imagine that the candidate believes that taxes should be lowered. She is likely to assert this argument in her speech, supporting it with examples proving why lowering taxes would benefit the public and how it could be accomplished. While the topic of the speech would be tax reform, the benefit of lowering taxes would be the **main idea**. Other candidates may have different perspectives on the topic; they may believe that higher taxes are necessary, or that current taxes are adequate. It is likely that their speeches, while on the same topic of tax reform, would have different main ideas: different arguments likewise supported by different examples. Determining what a speaker, writer, or text is asserting about a specific issue will reveal the main idea.

One more quick note: the CHSPE may also ask about a passage's **theme**, which is similar to but distinct from its topic. While a topic is usually a specific *person, place, thing,* or *issue,* the theme is an *idea* or *concept* that the author refers back to frequently. Examples of common themes include ideas like the importance of family, the dangers of technology, and the beauty of nature.

There will be many questions on the CHSPE that require you to differentiate between the topic, theme, and main idea of a passage. Let's look at an example passage to see how you would answer these questions.

> **Example:** "Babe Didrikson Zaharias, one of the most decorated female athletes of the twentieth century, is an inspiration for everyone. Born in 1911 in Beaumont, Texas, Zaharias lived in a time when women were considered second-class to men, but she never let that stop her from becoming a champion. Babe was one of seven children in a poor immigrant family, and was competitive from an early age. As a child she excelled at most things she tried, especially sports, which continued into high school and beyond. After high school, Babe played amateur basketball for two years, and soon after began training in track and field. Despite the fact that women were only allowed to enter in three events, Babe represented the United States in the

1932 Los Angeles Olympics, and won two gold medals and one silver for track and field events.

"In the early 1930s, Babe began playing golf which earned her a legacy. The first tournament she entered was a men's only tournament, however she did not make the cut to play. Playing golf as an amateur was the only option for a woman at this time, since there was no professional women's league. Babe played as an amateur for a little over a decade, until she turned pro in 1947 for the Ladies Professional Golf Association (LPGA) of which she was a founding member. During her career as a golfer, Babe won eighty-two tournaments, amateur and professional, including the U.S. Women's Open, All-American Open, and British Women's Open Golf Tournament. In 1953, Babe was diagnosed with cancer, but fourteen weeks later, she played in a tournament. That year she won her third U.S. Women's Open. However by 1955, she didn't have the physicality to compete anymore, and she died of the disease in 1956."

Determining the main idea, however, requires a little more analysis. The passage describes Babe Zaharias' life, but the main idea of the paragraph is what it says about her life. To figure out the main idea, consider what the writer is saying about Babe Zaharias. The writer is saying that she's someone to admire—that's the main idea and what unites all the information in the paragraph. Lastly, what might the theme of the passage be? The writer refers to several broad concepts, including never giving up and overcoming the odds, both of which could be themes for the passage. Two major indicators of the main idea of a paragraph or passage follow below:

- It is a general idea; it applies to all the more specific ideas in the passage. Every other sentence in a paragraph should be able to relate in some way to the main idea.

- It asserts a specific viewpoint that the author supports with facts, opinions, or other details. In other words, the main idea takes a stand.

Example: "From so far away it's easy to imagine the surface of our solar system's planets as enigmas—how could we ever know what those far-flung planets really look like? It turns out, however, that scientists have a number of tools at their disposal that allow them to paint detailed pictures of many planets' surfaces. The topography of Venus, for example, has been explored by several space probes, including the Russian Venera landers and NASA's Magellan orbiter. These craft used imaging and radar to map the surface of the planet, identifying a whole host of features including volcanoes, craters, and a complex system of channels. Mars has similarly been mapped by space probes, including the famous Mars Rovers, which are automated vehicles that actually landed on the surface of Mars. These rovers have been used by NASA and other space agencies to study the geology, climate, and possible biology of the planet.

"In addition these long-range probes, NASA has also used its series of orbiting telescopes to study distant planets. These four massively powerful telescopes include the famous Hubble Space Telescope as well as the Compton Gamma Ray Observatory, Chandra X-Ray Observatory, and the Spitzer Space Telescope. Scientists can use these telescopes to examine planets using not only visible light but also infrared and near-infrared light, ultraviolet light, x-rays and gamma rays.

"Powerful telescopes aren't just found in space: NASA makes use of Earth-bound telescopes as well. Scientists at the National Radio Astronomy Observatory in Charlottesville, VA, have spent decades using radio imaging to build an incredibly detailed portrait of Venus' surface. In fact, Earth-bound telescopes offer a distinct advantage over orbiting telescopes because they allow scientists to capture data from a fixed point, which in turn allows them to effectively compare data collected over long period of time."

Which of the following sentences best describes the main of the passage?
  a) It's impossible to know what the surfaces of other planets are really like.
  b) Telescopes are an important tool for scientists studying planets in our solar system.
  c) Venus' surface has many of the same features as the Earth's, including volcanoes, craters, and channels.
  d) Scientists use a variety of advanced technologies to study the surface of the planets in our solar system.

Answer a) can be eliminated because it directly contradicts the rest of the passage, which goes into detail about how scientists have learned about the surfaces of other planets. Answers b) and c) can also be eliminated because they offer only specific details from the passage—while both choices contain details from the passage, neither is general enough to encompass the passage as a whole. Only answer d) provides an assertion that is both backed up by the passage's content and general enough to cover the entire passage.

Topic and Summary Sentences

The main idea of a paragraph usually appears within the topic sentence. The **topic sentence** introduces the main idea to readers; it indicates not only the topic of a passage, but also the writer's perspective on the topic.

The first sentence in the Babe Zaharias text states the main idea: *Babe Didrikson Zaharias, one of the most decorated female athletes of the twentieth century, is an inspiration for everyone.*
Even though paragraphs generally begin with topic sentences due to their introductory nature, on occasion writers build up to the topic sentence by using supporting details in order to generate interest or build an argument. Be alert for paragraphs when writers do not include a clear topic sentence at all; even without a clear topic sentence, a paragraph will still have a main idea. You may also see a **summary sentence** at the end of a passage. As its name suggests, this sentence sums up the passage, often by restating the main idea and the author's key evidence supporting it.

Example: In the following paragraph, what are the topic and summary sentences?

"The Constitution of the United States establishes a series of limits to rein in centralized power. Separation of powers distributes federal authority among three competing branches: the executive, the legislative, and the judicial. Checks and balances allow the branches to check the usurpation of power by any one branch. States' rights are protected under the Constitution from too much encroachment by the federal government. Enumeration of powers names the specific and few powers the federal government has. These four restrictions have helped sustain the American republic for over two centuries."

The topic sentence is the first sentence in the paragraph. It introduces the topic of discussion, in this case the constitutional limits aimed at resisting centralized power. The summary sentence is the last sentence in the paragraph. It sums up the information that was just presented: here, that constitutional limits have helped sustain the United States of America for over two hundred years.

Implied Main Idea

When there's no clear topic sentence, you're looking for an **implied main idea**. This requires some detective work: you will need to look at the author's word choice and tone in addition to the content of the passage to find his or her main idea. Let's look at an example paragraph.

Example: "One of my summer reading books was *Mockingjay*. Though it's several hundred pages long, I read it in just a few days *I was captivated by the adventures of the main character and the complicated plot of the book. However, I felt like the ending didn't reflect the excitement of the story. Given what a powerful personality the main character has, I felt like the ending didn't do her justice.*"

Even without a clear topic sentence, this paragraph has a main idea. What is the writer's perspective on the book—what is the writer saying about it?
   a) *Mockingjay* is a terrific novel.
   b) *Mockingjay* is disappointing.
   c) *Mockingjay* is full of suspense.
   d) *Mockingjay* is a lousy novel.

The correct answer is B): the novel is disappointing. The process of elimination will reveal the correct answer if that is not immediately clear. While that the paragraph begins with positive commentary on the book—*I was captivated by the adventures of the main character and the complicated plot of the book*—this positive idea is followed by the contradictory transition word *however*. A) cannot be the correct answer because the author concludes that the novel was poor. Likewise, D) cannot be correct because it does not encompass all the ideas in the paragraph;

despite the negative conclusion, the author enjoyed most of the book. The main idea should be able to encompass all of the thoughts in a paragraph; choice D) does not apply to the beginning of this paragraph. Finally, choice C) is too specific; it could only apply to the brief description of the plot and adventures of the main character. That leaves choice B) as the best option. The author initially enjoyed the book, but was disappointed by the ending, which seemed unworthy of the exciting plot and character.

Example: "Fortunately, none of Alyssa's coworkers has ever seen inside the large filing drawer in her desk. Disguised by the meticulous neatness of the rest of her workspace, there was no sign of the chaos beneath. To even open it, she had to struggle for several minutes with the enormous pile of junk jamming the drawer, until it would suddenly give way, and papers, folders, and candy wrappers spilled out of the top and onto the floor. It was an organizational nightmare, with torn notes and spreadsheets haphazardly thrown on top of each other, and melted candy smeared across pages. She was worried the odor would soon permeate to her coworker's desks, revealing to them her secret."

Which sentence best describes the main idea of the paragraph above?
   a) Alyssa wishes she could move to a new desk.
   b) Alyssa wishes she had her own office.
   c) Alyssa is glad none of her coworkers know about her messy drawer.
   d) Alyssa is sad because she doesn't have any coworkers.

Clearly, Alyssa has a messy drawer, and C) is the right answer. The paragraph begins by indicating her gratitude that her coworkers do not know about her drawer (*Fortunately, none of Alyssa's coworkers has ever seen inside the large filing drawer in her desk.*) Plus, notice how the drawer is described: *it was an organizational nightmare*, and it apparently doesn't even function properly: *to even open the drawer, she had to struggle for several minutes.* The writer reveals that it has an odor, with *melted candy* inside. Alyssa is clearly ashamed of her drawer and fearful of being judged by her coworkers for it.

Supporting Details

Supporting details provide more support for the author's main idea. For instance, in the Babe Zaharias example above, the writer makes the general assertion that *Babe Didrikson Zaharias, one of the most decorated female athletes of the twentieth century, is an inspiration for everyone.* The rest of the paragraph provides supporting details with facts showing why she is an inspiration: the names of the illnesses she overcame, and the specific years she competed in the Olympics.

Be alert for **signal words**, which can be helpful in identifying supporting details. Signal words can also help you rule out sentences that are too broad to be the main idea or topic sentence: if a sentence begins with a signal word, it will likely be too specific to be a main idea.

Questions on the CHSPE will ask you to do two things with supporting details: you will need to find details that support a particular idea and also explain why a particular detail was included in the passage. In order to answer these questions, you need to have a solid understanding of the passage's main idea. With this knowledge, you can determine how a supporting detail fits in with the larger structure of the passage.

> **Example:** "From so far away it's easy to imagine the surface of our solar system's planets as enigmas—how could we ever know what those far-flung planets really look like? It turns out, however, that scientists have a number of tools at their disposal that allow them to paint detailed pictures of many planets' surfaces. The topography of Venus, for example, has been explored by several space probes, including the Russian *Venera* landers and NASA's *Magellan* orbiter. These craft used imaging and radar to map the surface of the planet, identifying a whole host of features including volcanoes, craters, and a complex system of channels. Mars has similarly been mapped by space probes, including the famous Mars Rovers, which are automated vehicles that actually landed on the surface of Mars. These rovers have been used by NASA and other space agencies to study the geology, climate, and possible biology of the planet.
>
> "In addition these long-range probes, NASA has also used its series of orbiting telescopes to study distant planets. These four massively powerful telescopes include the famous Hubble Space Telescope as well as the Compton Gamma Ray Observatory, Chandra X-Ray Observatory, and the Spitzer Space Telescope. Scientists can use these telescopes to examine planets using not only visible light but also infrared and near-infrared light, ultraviolet light, x-rays and gamma rays. "Powerful telescopes aren't just found in space: NASA makes use of Earth-bound telescopes as well. Scientists at the National Radio Astronomy Observatory in Charlottesville, VA, have spent decades using radio imaging to build an incredibly detailed portrait of Venus' surface. In fact, Earth-bound telescopes offer a distinct advantage over orbiting telescopes because they allow scientists to capture data from a fixed point, which in turn allows them to effectively compare data collected over long period of time."

Which sentence from the text best helps develop the idea that scientists make use of many different technologies to study the surfaces of other planets?

a) These rovers have been used by NASA and other space agencies to study the geology, climate, and possible biology of the planet.

b) From so far away it's easy to imagine the surface of our solar system's planets as enigmas—how could we ever know what those far-flung planets really look like?

c) In addition these long-range probes, NASA has also used its series of orbiting telescopes to study distant planets.

d) These craft used imaging and radar to map the surface of the planet, identifying a whole host of features including volcanoes, craters, and a complex system of channels.

You're looking for detail from the passage that supports the main idea—scientists make use of many different technologies to study the surfaces of other planets. Answer a) includes a specific detail about rovers, but does not offer any details that support the idea of multiple technologies being used. Similarly, answer d) provides another specific detail about space probes. Answer b) doesn't provide any supporting details; it simply introduces the topic of the passage. Only answer c) provides a detail that directly supports the author's assertion that scientists use multiple technologies to study the planets.

If true, which detail could be added to the passage above to support the author's argument that scientists use many different technologies to study the surface of planets?

a) Because the Earth's atmosphere blocks x-rays, gamma rays, and infrared radiation, NASA needed to put telescopes in orbit above the atmosphere.

b) In 2015, NASA released a map of Venus which was created by compiling images from orbiting telescopes and long-range space probes.

c) NASA is currently using the *Curiosity* and *Opportunity* rovers to look for signs of ancient life on Mars.

d) NASA has spent over $2.5 billion to build, launch, and repair the Hubble Space Telescope.

You can eliminate answers c) and d) because they don't address the topic of studying the surface of planets. Answer a) can also be eliminated because it only addresses a single technology. Only choice b) provides would add support to the author's claim about the importance of using multiple technologies.

The author likely included the detail *Earth-bound telescopes offer a distinct advantage over orbiting telescopes because they allow scientists to capture data from a fixed point* in order to:

   a) Explain why it has taken scientists so long to map the surface of Venus.
   b) Suggest that Earth-bound telescopes are the most important equipment used by NASA scientists.
   c) Prove that orbiting telescopes will soon be replaced by Earth-bound telescopes.
   d) Demonstrate why NASA scientists rely on my different types of scientific equipment.

Only answer d) directs directly to the author's main argument. The author doesn't mention how long it has taken to map the surface of Venus (answer a), nor does he say that one technology is more important than the others (answer b). And while this detail does highlight the advantages of using Earth-bound telescopes, the author's argument is that many technologies are being used at the same time, so there's no reason to think that orbiting telescopes will be replaced (answer c).

Text Structure

Authors can structure passages in a number of different ways. These distinct organizational patterns, referred to as **text structure**, use the logical relationships between ideas to improve the readability and coherence of a text. The most common ways passages are organized include:

- **problem-solution**: the author presents a problem and then discusses a solution

- **comparison-contrast**: the author presents two situations and then discusses the similarities and differences

- **cause-effect**: the author presents an action and then discusses the resulting effects

- **descriptive**: an idea, object, person, or other item is described in detail

Example: "The issue of public transportation has begun to haunt the fast-growing cities of the southern United States. Unlike their northern counterparts, cities like Atlanta, Dallas, and Houston have long promoted growth out and not up—these are cities full of sprawling suburbs and single-family homes, not densely concentrated skyscrapers and apartments. What to do then, when all those suburbanites need to get into the central business districts for work? For a long time it seemed highways were the answer: twenty-lane wide expanses of concrete that would allow commuters to move from home to work and back again. But these modern miracles have become time-sucking, pollution spewing nightmares. They may not like it, but it's time for these cities to turn toward public transport like trains and buses if they want their cities to remain livable."

The organization of this passage can best be described as:

    a) a comparison of two similar ideas
    b) a description of a place
    c) a discussion of several effects all related to the same cause
    d) a discussion of a problem followed by the suggestion of a solution

You can exclude answer choice c) because the author provides no root cause or a list of effects. From there this question gets tricky, because the passage contains structures similar to those described above. For example, it compares two things (cities in the North and South) and describes a place (a sprawling city). However, if you look at the overall organization of the passage, you can see that it starts by presenting a problem (transportation) and then presents a solution (trains and buses), making answer d) the only choice that encompasses the entire passage.

The Author's Purpose

Whenever an author writes a text, she always has a purpose, whether that's to entertain, inform, explain, or persuade. A short story, for example, is meant to entertain, while an online news article would be designed to inform the public about a current event.

Each of these different types of writing has a specific name. On the CHSPE, you will be asked to identify which of these categories a passage fits into:

- **Narrative writing** tells a story. (novel, short story, play)

- **Expository writing** informs people. (newspaper and magazine articles)

- **Technical writing** explains something. (product manual, directions)

- **Persuasive writing** tries to convince the reader of something. (opinion column on a blog)

You may also be asked about primary and secondary sources. These terms describe not the writing itself but the author's relationship to what's being written about. A **primary source** is an unaltered piece of writing that was composed during the time when the events being described took place; these texts are often written by the people involved. A **secondary source** might address the same topic but provides extra commentary or analysis. These texts can be written by people not directly involved in the events. For example, a book written by a political candidate to inform people about his or her stand on an issue is a primary source; an online article written by a journalist analyzing how that position will affect the election is a secondary source.

Example: "Elizabeth closed her eyes and braced herself on the armrests that divided her from her fellow passengers. Take-off was always the worst part for her. The revving of the engines, the way her stomach dropped as the plane lurched upward:

17

it made her feel sick. Then, she had to watch the world fade away beneath her, getting smaller and smaller until it was just her and the clouds hurtling through the sky. Sometimes (but only sometimes) it just had to be endured, though. She focused on the thought of her sister's smiling face and her new baby nephew as the plane slowly pulled onto the runway."

The passage above is reflective of which type of writing?
   a) Narrative
   b) Expository
   c) Technical
   d) Persuasive

The passage is telling a story—we meet Elizabeth and learn about her fear of flying—so it's a narrative text (answer a). There is no factual information presented or explained, nor is the author trying to persuade the reader.

Facts vs. Opinions

On the CHSPE Reading passages you might be asked to identify a statement in a passage as either a fact or an opinion, so you'll need to know the difference between the two. A **fact** is a statement or thought that can be proven to be true. The statement *Wednesday comes after Tuesday* is a fact—you can point to a calendar to prove it. In contrast, an **opinion** is an assumption that is not based in fact and cannot be proven to be true. The assertion that *television is more entertaining than feature films* is an opinion—people will disagree on this, and there's no reference you can use to prove or disprove it.

> **Example:**
> "Exercise is critical for healthy development in children. Today, there is an epidemic of unhealthy children in the United States who will face health problems in adulthood due to poor diet and lack of exercise as children. This is a problem for all Americans, especially with the rising cost of healthcare.
> "It is vital that school systems and parents encourage their children to engage in a minimum of thirty minutes of cardiovascular exercise each day, mildly increasing their heart rate for a sustained period. This is proven to decrease the likelihood of developmental diabetes, obesity, and a multitude of other health problems. Also, children need a proper diet rich in fruits and vegetables so that they can grow and develop physically, as well as learn healthy eating habits early on."

Which of the following is a fact in the passage, not an opinion?
   a) Fruits and vegetables are the best way to help children be healthy.
   b) Children today are lazier than they were in previous generations.
   c) The risk of diabetes in children is reduced by physical activity.
   d) Children should engage in thirty minutes of exercise a day.

Choice b) can be discarded immediately because it is negative and is not discussed anywhere in the passage. Answers a) and d) are both opinions—the author is promoting exercise, fruits, and vegetables as a way to make children healthy. (Notice that these incorrect answers contain words that hint at being an opinion such as *best*, *should*, or other comparisons.) Answer b), on the other hand, is a simple fact stated by the author; it's introduced by the word *proven* to indicate that you don't need to just take the author's word for it.

Drawing Conclusions

In addition to understanding the main idea and factual content of a passage, you'll also be asked to take your analysis one step further and anticipate what other information could logically be added to the passage. In a non-fiction passage, for example, you might be asked which statement the author of the passage would agree with. In an excerpt from a fictional work, you might be asked to anticipate what the character would do next.

To answer these questions, you need to have a solid understanding of the topic, theme, and main idea of the passage; armed with this information, you can figure out which of the answer choices best fits within those criteria (or alternatively, which ones do not). For example, if the author of the passage is advocating for safer working conditions in textile factories, any supporting details that would be added to the passage should support that idea. You might add sentences that contain information about the number of accidents that occur in textile factories or that outline a new plan for fire safety.

Example: "Today, there is an epidemic of unhealthy children in the United States who will face health problems in adulthood due to poor diet and lack of exercise during their childhood. This is a problem for all Americans, as adults with chronic health issues are adding to the rising cost of healthcare. A child who grows up living an unhealthy lifestyle is likely to become an adult who does the same.
"Because exercise is critical for healthy development in children, it is vital that school systems and parents encourage their children to engage in a minimum of thirty minutes of cardiovascular exercise each day. Even this small amount of exercise has been proven to decrease the likelihood that young people will develop diabetes, obesity, and other health issues as adults. In addition to exercise, children need a proper diet rich in fruits and vegetables so that they can grow and develop physically. Starting a good diet early also teaches children healthy eating habits they will carry into adulthood."

The author of this passage would most likely agree with which statement?
   a) Parents are solely responsible for the health of their children.
   b) Children who do not want to exercise should not be made to.
   c) Improved childhood nutrition will help lower the amount Americans spend on healthcare.
   d) It's not important to teach children healthy eating habits because they will learn them as adults.

The author would most likely support answer c): he mentions in the first paragraph that unhealthy habits are adding to the rising cost of healthcare. The main idea of the passage is that nutrition and exercise are important for children, so answer b) doesn't make sense—the author would likely support measures to encourage children to exercise. Answers a) and d) can also be eliminated because they are directly contradicted in the text. The author specifically mentions the role of schools systems, so he doesn't believe parents are solely responsible for their children's health. He also specifically states that children who grow up with unhealthy habit will become adults with unhealthy habits, which contradicts d).

Example: "Elizabeth closed her eyes and braced herself on the armrests that divided her from her fellow passengers. Take-off was always the worst part for her. The revving of the engines, the way her stomach dropped as the plane lurched upward: it made her feel sick. Then, she had to watch the world fade away beneath her, getting smaller and smaller until it was just her and the clouds hurtling through the sky. Sometimes (but only sometimes) it just had to be endured, though. She focused on the thought of her sister's smiling face and her new baby nephew as the plane slowly pulled onto the runway."

Which of the following is Elizabeth least likely to do in the future?
   a) Take a flight to her brother's wedding.
   b) Apply for a job as a flight attendant.
   c) Never board an airplane again.
   d) Get sick on an airplane.

It's clear from the passage that Elizabeth hates flying, but it willing to endure it for the sake of visiting her family. Thus, it seems likely that she would be willing to get on a plane for her brother's wedding, making a) and c) incorrect answers. The passage also explicitly tells us that she feels sick on planes, so d) is likely to happen. We can infer, though, that she would not enjoy being on an airplane for work, so she's very unlikely to apply for a job as a flight attendant, which is choice b).

VOCABULARY

You may also be asked to provide definitions or intended meanings for words within passages. Some of those words, you may never have encountered before the test. But there are ways to answer correctly, and confidently, regardless!

Context Clues

The most fundamental vocabulary skill is using the context of a word to determine its meaning. Your ability to observe sentences closely is extremely useful when it comes to understanding new vocabulary words.

Types of Context

There are two different types of context that can bring understanding to the meaning of unfamiliar words: **sentence context** and **situational context**. Regardless of which context is present, these types of questions are not really testing your knowledge of vocabulary; rather, they test your ability to comprehend the meaning of a word through its usage.

> **Situational context** is context that comes from understanding the situation in which a word or phrase occurs.

> **Sentence context** occurs within the sentence that contains the vocabulary word. To figure out words using sentence context clues, you should first determine the most important words in the sentence.

> > **Example:** I had a hard time reading her <u>illegible</u> handwriting.
> > a) Neat.
> > b) Unsafe.
> > c) Sloppy.
> > d) Educated.

> Already, you know that this sentence is discussing something that is hard to read. Look at the word that **illegible** is describing: **handwriting**. Based on context clues, you can tell that illegible means that her handwriting is hard to read.

> Next, look at the answer choices. Choice **a) Neat** is obviously a wrong answer because neat handwriting would not be difficult to read. Choice **b) Unsafe** and **d) Educated** don't make sense. Therefore, choice **c) Sloppy** is the best answer choice.

Types of Clues

There are four types of clues that can help you understand context, and therefore the meaning of a word. They are **restatement**, **positive/negative**, **contrast**, and **specific detail**.

> **Restatement** clues occur when the definition of the word is clearly stated in the sentence.

Example: The dog was <u>dauntless</u> in the face of danger, braving the fire to save the girl.
  a) Difficult.
  b) Fearless.
  c) Imaginative.

Demonstrating **bravery** in the face of danger would be **fearless, choice b)**. In this case, the context clues tell you exactly what the word means.

Positive/negative clues can tell you whether a word has a positive or negative meaning.

Example: The magazine gave a great review of the fashion show, stating the clothing was **sublime**.
  a) Horrible.
  b) Exotic.
  c) Bland
  d) Gorgeous.

The sentence tells us that the author liked the clothing enough to write a **great** review, so the best answer choice will be a positive word. Therefore, you can immediately rule out choices **a)** and **c)** because they are negative words. **Exotic** is a neutral word; alone, it doesn't inspire a **great** review. The most positive word is gorgeous, which makes choice **d) Gorgeous** the best answer.

The following sentence uses both restatement and positive/negative clues:

> "Janet suddenly found herself <u>destitute</u>, so poor she could barely afford to eat."

The second part of the sentence clearly indicates that destitute is a negative word; it also restates the meaning: very poor.

Contrast clues include the opposite meaning of a word. Words like **but, on the other hand**, and **however** are tip-offs that a sentence contains a contrast clue.

Example: Beth did not spend any time preparing for the test, but Tyron kept a <u>rigorous</u> study schedule.

    a) Strict.
    b) Loose.
    c) Boring.
    d) Strange.

In this case, the word **but** tells us that Tyron studied in a different way than Beth. If Beth did not study very hard, then Tyron did study hard for the test. The best answer here, therefore, is choice **a) Strict**.

Specific detail clues give a precise detail that illuminate the word's meaning.

Example: The box was heavier than he expected and it began to become <u>cumbersome</u>.

    a) Impossible.
    b) Burdensome.
    c) Obligated.
    d) Easier.

Start by looking at the specific details of the sentence. Choice **d)** can be eliminated right away because it is doubtful it would become **easier** to carry something that is **heavier**. There are also no clues in the sentence to indicate he was **obligated** to carry the box, so choice **c)** can also be disregarded. The sentence specifics, however, do tell you that the package was cumbersome because it was heavy to carry; this is a burden, which is **burdensome**, choice **b)**.

It is important to remember that more than one of these clues can be present in the same sentence. The more there are, the easier it will be to determine the meaning of the word, so look for them.

Denotation and Connotation

As you know, many English words have more than one meaning. For example, the word **quack** has two distinct definitions: the sound a duck makes; and a person who publicly pretends to have a skill, knowledge, education, or qualification which they do not possess.

The **denotations** of a word are the dictionary definitions.

The **connotations** of a word are the implied meaning(s) or emotion which the word makes you think.

Example: "Sure," Pam said excitedly, "I'd just love to join your club; it sounds so exciting!"

Now, read this sentence:

"Sure," Pam said sarcastically, "I'd just love to join your club; it sounds so exciting!"

Even though the two sentences only differ by one word, they have completely different meanings. The difference, of course, lies in the words "excitedly" and "sarcastically."

Prefixes, Roots, and Suffixes

Although you are not expected to know every word in the English language for your test, you will need to have the ability to use deductive reasoning to find the choice that is the best match for the word in question, which is why we are going to explain how to break a word into its parts of meaning.

prefix – root – suffix

One trick in dividing a word into its parts is to first divide the word into its **syllables**. To show how syllables can help you find roots and affixes, we'll use the word **descendant,** which means one who comes from an ancestor. Start by dividing the word into its individual syllables; this word has three:

de-scend-ant.

The next step is to look at the beginning and end of the word, and then determine if these syllables are prefixes, suffixes, or possible roots. You can then use the meanings of each part to guide you in defining the word. When you divide words into their specific parts, they do not always add up to an exact definition, but you will see a relationship between their parts.

Note: This trick won't always work in every situation, because not all prefixes, roots, and suffixes have only one syllable. For example, take the word **monosyllabic** (which ironically means "one syllable"). There are five syllables in that word, but only three parts. The prefix is "mono," meaning "one." The root "syllab" refers to "syllable," while the suffix "ic" means "pertaining to." Therefore, we have – very ironically – one extremely long word which means "pertaining to one syllable."

Roots
Roots are the building blocks of all words. Every word is either a root itself or has a root. Just as a plant cannot grow without roots, neither can vocabulary, because a word must have a root to give it meaning.

Example: The test instructions were **unclear.**

The root is what is left when you strip away all the prefixes and suffixes from a word. In this case, take away the prefix "un-," and you have the root **clear**.

Roots are not always recognizable words, because they generally come from Latin or Greek words, such as **nat**, a Latin root meaning **born**. The word native, which means a person born of a referenced placed, comes from this root, so does the word prenatal, meaning before birth. Yet, if you used the prefix **nat** instead of born, just on its own, no one would know what you were talking about.

Words can also have more than one root. For example, the word **omnipotent** means all powerful. Omnipotent is a combination of the roots **omni-**, meaning all or every, and -**potent**, meaning power or strength. In this case, **omni** cannot be used on its own as a single word, but **potent** can.

Again, it is important to keep in mind that roots do not always match the exact definitions of words and they can have several different spellings, but breaking a word into its parts is still one of the best ways to determine its meaning.

Prefixes
A **Prefix** is a syllable(s) added to the beginning of a word, while **suffixes** are syllables added to the end of the word. Both carry assigned meanings. The common name for prefixes and suffixes is **affixes**. Affixes do not have to be attached directly to a root and a word can often have more than one prefix and/or suffix.

Prefixes and suffixes can be attached to a word to completely change the word's meaning or to enhance the word's original meaning. Although they don't mean much to us on their own, when attached to other words affixes can make a world of difference.

The word **prefix** itself can serve as an example:

Fix means to place something securely; and **Pre** means before. Therefore, **Prefix** means to place something before or in front.

Suffixes
Suffixes come after the root of a word.

Example: Feminism.

Femin is a root. It means female, woman. **-ism** means act, practice or process. **Feminism** is the defining and establishing of equal political, economic, and social rights for women.

Unlike prefixes, **suffixes** can be used to change a word's part of speech.

Example: "Randy raced to the finish line." VS "Shana's costume was very racy."

In the first sentence, raced is a verb. In the second sentence, racy is an adjective. By changing the suffix from **-ed** to **-y**, the word race changes from a verb into an adjective, which has an entirely different meaning.

Although you cannot determine the meaning of a word by a prefix or suffix alone, you *can* use your knowledge of what root words mean to eliminate answer choices; indicating if the word is positive or negative can give you a partial meaning of the word.

Test Your Knowledge: Language Arts – The Reading Section

Read the following passages and answer the questions that correspond with each passage:

The Flu

Influenza, or the flu, has historically been one of the most common and deadliest human sicknesses. While many people who contract this virus will recover, others will not. Over the past 150 years, tens of millions of people have died from the flu, and millions more have been left with lingering complications including secondary infections.

Although it's a common disease, the flu is actually not highly infectious; that is, it is relatively difficult to contract. The virus can only be transmitted when individuals come into direct contact with the bodily fluids of people infected with it, often when they are exposed to expelled aerosol particles resulting from coughing and sneezing. Since these particles only travel short distances and the virus will die within a few hours on hard surfaces, it can be contained with simple health measures like hand washing and face masks. However, the spread of this disease can only be contained when people are aware that such measures must be taken. One of the reasons the flu has historically been so deadly is the window of time between a person's infection and the development of symptoms. Viral shedding—when the body releases a virus that has been successfully reproducing in it— takes place two days after infection, while symptoms do not usually develop until the third day. Thus, infected individuals may unknowingly infect others for least twenty-four hours before developing symptoms themselves.

1. What is the main idea of the passage?
    a) The flu is a deadly disease that's difficult to control because people become infectious before they show symptoms.
    b) In order for the flu to be transmitted, individuals must come in contact with bodily fluids from infected individuals.
    c) The spread of flu is easy to contain because the virus does not live long either as aerosol particles or on hard surfaces.
    d) The flu has killed tens of millions of people and can often cause deadly secondary infections.

2. Why isn't the flu considered to be highly infectious?
    a) Many people who get the flu will recover and have no lasting complications, so only a small number of people who become infected will die.
    b) The process of viral shedding takes two days, so infected individuals have enough time to implement simple health measures that stop the spread of the disease.
    c) The flu virus cannot travel far or live for long periods of time outside the human body, so its spread can easily be contained if measures are taken.
    d) Twenty-four hours is a relatively short period of time for the virus to spread among a population.

3. Which of the following correctly describes the flu?

a) The flu is easy to contract and always fatal.
b) The flu is difficult to contract and always fatal.
c) The flu is easy to contract and sometimes fatal.
d) The flu is difficult to contract and sometimes fatal.

4. Which statement is not a detail from the passage?
   a) Tens of millions of people have been killed by the flu virus.
   b) There is typically a twenty-four hour window during which individuals are infectious but not showing flu symptoms.
   c) Viral shedding is the process by which people recover from the flu.
   d) The flu can be transmitted by direct contact with bodily fluids from infected individuals or by exposure to aerosol particles.

5. What is the meaning of the word *measures* in the last paragraph?
   a) a plan of action
   b) a standard unit
   c) an adequate amount
   d) a rhythmic movement

6. What can the reader conclude from the passage above?
   a) Preemptively implementing health measures like hand washing and face masks could help stop the spread of the flu virus.
   b) Doctors are not sure how the flu virus is transmitted, so they are unsure how to stop it from spreading.
   c) The flu is dangerous because it is both deadly and highly infectious.
   d) Individuals stop being infectious three days after they are infected.

Snakes

Skin coloration and markings play an important role in the world of snakes. Those intricate diamonds, stripes, and swirls help these animals hide from predators and attract mates. Perhaps most importantly (for us humans, anyway), the markings can also indicate whether a snake is venomous. While it might seem counterintuitive for a poisonous snake to stand out in bright red or blue, that fancy costume tells any approaching predator that eating it would be a bad idea.

If you see a flashy-looking snake out the woods, though, those markings don't necessarily mean it's poisonous: some snakes have a found a way to ward off predators without the actual venom. The California king snake, for example, has very similar markings to the venomous coral snake with whom it frequently shares a habitat. However, the king snake is actually nonvenomous; it's merely pretending to be dangerous to eat. A predatory hawk or eagle, usually hunting from high in the sky, can't tell the difference between the two species, so the king snake gets passed over and lives another day.

7. What is the author's primary purpose in writing this essay?
   a) to explain how the markings on a snake are related to whether it is venomous
   b) to teach readers the difference between coral snakes and king snakes

c) to illustrate why snakes are dangerous
d) to demonstrate how animals survive in difficult environments

8. What can the reader conclude from the passage above?
   a) The king snake is dangerous to humans.
   b) The coral snake and the king snake are both hunted by the same predators.
   c) It's safe to handle snakes in the woods because you can easily tell whether they're poisonous.
   d) The king snake changes its markings when hawks or eagles are close by.

9. What is the best summary of this passage?
   a) Humans can use coloration and markings to determine whether snakes are poisonous.
   b) Animals often use coloration and markings to attract mates and warn predators that they're poisonous.
   c) The California king snake and coral snake have nearly identical markings.
   d) Venomous snakes often have bright markings, although nonvenomous snakes can also mimic those colors.

10. Which statement is not a detail from the passage?
    a) Predators will avoid eating king snakes because their markings are similar to those on coral snakes.
    b) King snakes and coral snakes live in the same habitats.
    c) The coral snake uses its coloration to hide from predators.
    d) The king snake is not venomous.

11. What is the meaning of the word *intricate* in the first paragraph?
    a) complicated
    b) colorful
    c) purposeful
    d) changeable

12. What is the difference between king snakes and coral snakes according to the passage?
    a) Both king snakes and coral snakes are nonvenomous, but coral snakes have colorful markings.
    b) Both king snakes and coral snakes are venomous, but king snakes have colorful markings.
    c) King snakes are nonvenomous, while coral snakes are venomous.
    d) Coral snakes are nonvenomous, while king snakes are venomous.

Taking Temperatures

Taking a person's temperature is one of the most basic and common health care tasks. Everyone from nurses to emergency medical technicians to concerned parents has needed to grab a thermometer and take somebody's temperature. But what is the best way to get an accurate reading? The answer depends on the situation.

The most common way people measure body temperature is orally. A simple digital or disposable thermometer is placed under the tongue for a few minutes, and the task is complete. There are many situations, however, when measuring temperature orally isn't an option. For example, when a person can't breathe through his nose, he won't be able to keep his mouth closed long enough to get an accurate reading. In these situations, it's often preferable to place the thermometer in the rectum or armpit. In addition, using the rectum provides a much more accurate reading than any other location does.

It's also often the case that certain people, like agitated patients or fussy babies, won't be able to sit still long enough for an accurate reading. In these situations, it's best to use a thermometer that works much more quickly, such as one that measures temperature in the ear or at the temporal artery. No matter which method is chosen, however, it's important to check the average temperature for each region, as it can vary by several degrees.

13. Which statement is not a detail from the passage?
    a) Taking someone's temperature in her ear or at her temporal artery is more accurate than taking it orally.
    b) If an individual cannot breathe through his nose, taking his temperature orally will likely result in an inaccurate reading.
    c) The standard human body temperature varies depending on whether it's measured in the mouth, rectum, armpit, ear, or temporal artery.
    d) The most common way to measure temperature is by placing a thermometer in the mouth.

14. What is the author's primary purpose in writing this essay?
    a) to advocate for the use of thermometers that measure temperature in the ear or at the temporal artery
    b) to explain the methods available to measure a person's temperature and the situations in which each method is appropriate
    c) to warn readers that the average temperature of the human body varies by region
    d) to discuss how nurses use different types of thermometers depending on the patient they are examining

15. What is the best summary of this passage?
   a) It's important that everyone knows the best way to take a person's temperature in any given situation.
   b) The most common method of taking a person's temperature—orally—isn't appropriate in some situations.
   c) The most accurate way to take a temperature is by placing a digital thermometer in the rectum.
   d) It's important to check a person's temperature in more than one region of the body.

16. What is the meaning of the word *agitated* in the last paragraph?
   a) obviously upset
   b) quickly moving
   c) violently ill
   d) slightly dirty

17. According to the passage, why is it sometimes preferable to take a person's temperature rectally?
   a) Rectal readings are more accurate than oral readings.
   b) Many people cannot sit still long enough to have their temperatures taken orally.
   c) Temperature readings can vary widely between regions of the body.
   d) Many people do not have access to fast-acting thermometers.

Credit Scores

Credit scores, which range from 300 to 850, are a single value that summarizes an individual's credit history. Pay your bills late? Your credit score will be lower than that of someone who gets their electric bill filed on the first of every month. Just paid off your massive student loans? You can expect your credit score to shoot up. The companies that compile credit scores actually keep track of all the loans, credit cards, and bill payments in your name. This massive amount of information is summed up in a credit report, which is then distilled to a single value: your credit score.

Credit scores are used by many institutions who need to evaluate the risk of providing loans, rentals, or services to individuals. Banks use credit scores when deciding when to approve loans; they can also use them to determine the terms of the loan itself. Similarly, car dealers, landlords, and credit card companies will likely all access your credit report before agreeing to do business with you. Even your employer can access a modified version of your credit report (although it will not have your actual credit score on it).

When it comes to credit, everyone begins with a clean slate. The first time you access any credit—be it a credit card, student loan, or rental agreement—information begins to accumulate in your credit report. For this reason, having no credit score can often be just as bad as having a low one. Lenders want to know that you have a history of borrowing money and paying it back on time. After all, if you've never taken out a loan, how can a bank know that you'll pay back its money? So, having nothing on your credit report can result in low credit limits and high interest rates.

With time, though, credit scores can be raised. With every payment, your credit report improves and banks will be more likely to loan you money. These new loans will in turn raise your score even further (as long as you keep making payments, of course).

In general, there are a number of basic steps you can take to raise your credit score. First, ensure that you make payments on time. When payments are past due, that not only has a negative impact on your score, but new creditors will also be reluctant to lend to you while you are delinquent on other accounts.

Being smart about taking on debt is another key factor in keeping your credit score high. As someone who is just starting off in the financial world, you will receive multiple offers to open accounts, say for an introductory credit card or short-term loan. You may also find that as your score increases, you get offers for larger and larger loans. (Predatory lenders are a scourge on the young as well as the old.) But just because banks are offering you those loans doesn't make them a good idea. Instead, you should only take on debt you know you can pay back in a reasonable amount of time.

Lastly, keep an eye on unpaid student loans, medical bills, and parking tickets, all of which can take a negative toll on your credit score. In fact, your credit score will take a major hit from any bill that's sent to a collection agency, so it's in your best interest to avoid letting bills get to that point. Many organizations will agree to keep bills away from collection agencies if you set up a fee-payment system.

18. Which of the following is an opinion stated in the passage?
   a) Credit scores, which range from 300 to 850, are a single value that summarizes an individual's credit history.
   b) Many organizations will agree to keep bills away from collection agencies if you set up a fee-payment system.
   c) After all, if you've never taken out a loan, how can a bank know that you'll pay back its money?
   d) Predatory lenders are a scourge on the young as well as the old.

19. What is the author's primary purpose in writing this essay?
   a) to help readers understand and improve their credit scores
   b) to warn banks about the dangers of lending to people with no credit score
   c) to persuade readers to take out large loans in order to improve their credit scores
   d) to explain to readers how the process of taking out a bank loan works

20. What is the best summary of this passage?
    a) Individuals with low credit scores will likely have trouble getting credit cards and loans. However, they can improve their credit scores over time.
    b) Having no credit score can often be worse than having a low credit score, so it's important to sign up for credit cards and loans early in life.
    c) Credit scores summarize an individual's credit history and are used by many businesses. They can be improved by making smart financial decisions.
    d) Credit scores can be raised by paying bills on time, taking out reasonably sized loans, and avoiding collection agencies.

21. What can the reader conclude from the passage above?
    a) It is possible to wipe your credit report clean and start over with a blank slate.
    b) A person with a large amount of debt can likely get a loan with a low interest rate because they have demonstrated they are trustworthy.
    c) Someone who has borrowed and paid back large sums of money will get a loan with more favorable terms than someone who has never borrowed money before.
    d) A college student with no credit cards or debt likely has a high credit score.

22. Which statement is not a detail from the passage?
    a) In general, there are a number of basic steps you can take to raise your credit score.
    b) When it comes to credit, everyone begins with a clean slate.
    c) Employers can access your credit score before hiring you.
    d) Predatory lenders are a scourge on the young as well as the old.

23. According to the passage, which individual is likely to have the highest credit score?
    a) someone who has had medical bills sent to a collection agency
    b) someone who is in the process of paying back his student loans
    c) someone who has never borrowed any money but pays his bills on time
    d) someone who has borrowed a large amount of money and paid it back on time

24. What is the meaning of the word *distilled* in the first paragraph?
    a) to refine to an essence
    b) to explain at length
    c) to keep records of
    d) to undergo substantial change

Hand Washing
Hand washing is one of our most powerful weapons against infection. The idea behind hand washing is deceptively simple. Many illnesses are spread when people touch infected surfaces, such as door handles or other people's hands, and then touch their own eyes, mouths, or noses. So, if pathogens can be removed from the hands before they spread, infections can be prevented. When done correctly, hand washing can prevent the spread of many dangerous bacteria and viruses, including those that cause the flu, the common cold, diarrhea, and many acute respiratory illnesses.

The most basic method of hand washing only involves soap and water. Just twenty seconds of scrubbing with soap and a through rinse with water is enough to kill and/or wash away many pathogens. The process doesn't even require warm water—studies have shown that cold water is just as effective at reducing the number of microbes on the hands. While antibacterial soaps are also available, soap and cold water is just as effective.

In recent years, hand sanitizers have become popular as an alternative to hand washing. These gels, liquids, and foams contain a high concentration of alcohol (usually at least sixty percent) which kills most bacteria and fungi; they can also be effective against some, but not all, viruses. There is a downside to hand sanitizer, however. Because the sanitizer isn't rinsed from hands, it only kills pathogens and does nothing to remove organic matter. So, hands "cleaned" with hand sanitizer may still harbor pathogens. Thus, while hand sanitizer can be helpful in situations where soap and clean water isn't available, a simple hand washing is still the best option.

25. What is the meaning of the word *harbor* in the last paragraph?
    a) to disguise
    b) to hide
    c) to wash away
    d) to give a home

26. Which of the following is not a fact stated in the passage?
    a) Many infections occur because people get pathogens on their hands and then touch their own eyes, mouths, or noses.
    b) Antibacterial soaps and warm water are the best way to remove pathogens from hands.
    c) Most hand sanitizers have a concentration of at least sixty percent alcohol.
    d) Hand sanitizer can be an acceptable alternative to hand washing when soap and water aren't available.

27. What is the best summary of this passage?
    a) Many diseases are spread by pathogens that can live on the hands. Hand washing is the best way to remove these pathogens and prevent disease.
    b) Simple hand washing can prevent the spread of many common illnesses, including the flu, the common cold, diarrhea, and many acute respiratory illnesses. Hand sanitizer can also kill the pathogens that cause these diseases.
    c) Simple hand washing with soap and cold water is an effective way to reduce the spread of disease. Antibacterial soaps and hand sanitizers may be also be used but are not significantly more effective.
    d) Using hand sanitizer will kill many pathogens, but it will not remove organic matter. Hand washing with soap and water is a better option when it is available.

28. Knowing that the temperature of the water does not change the effectiveness of hand washing, it can be concluded that water plays an important role in hand washing because it _____

    a) has antibacterial properties.
    b) physically removes pathogens from hands.
    c) cools hands to make them inhospitable for dangerous bacteria.
    d) is hot enough to kill bacteria.

29. What is the author's primary purpose in writing this essay?

    a) to persuade readers of the importance and effectiveness of hand washing with soap and cold water
    b) to dissuade readers from using hand sanitizer
    c) to explain how many common diseases are spread
    d) to describe the many health benefits of hand washing and using hand sanitizer

30. What can the reader conclude from the passage above?

    a) Hand washing would do little to limit infections that spread through particles in the air.
    b) Hand washing is not necessary for people who do not touch their eyes, mouths, or noses with their hands.
    c) Hand sanitizer serves no purpose and should not be used as an alternative to hand washing.
    d) Hand sanitizer will likely soon replace hand washing as the preferred method of removing pathogens from hands.

The Jazz Age

In recent decades, jazz has been associated with New Orleans and festivals like Mardi Gras, but in the 1920s jazz was a booming trend whose influence affected many aspects of American culture. In fact, the years between World War I and the Great Depression were known as the Jazz Age, a term coined by F. Scott Fitzgerald in his famous novel *The Great Gatsby*. Sometimes also called the Roaring Twenties, this time period saw major urban centers experiencing new economic, cultural, and artistic vitality. In the United States, musicians flocked to cities like New York and Chicago, which would became famous hubs for jazz musicians. Ella Fitzgerald, for example, moved from Virginia to New York City to begin her much-lauded singing career, and jazz pioneer Louis Armstrong got his big break in Chicago.

Jazz music was played by and for a more expressive and freed populace than the United States had previously seen. Women had recently gained the right to vote and were publicly drinking and dancing to jazz music. This period marked the emergence of the *flapper*, a woman determined to make a statement about her new role in society. Jazz music also provided the soundtrack for the explosion of African American art and culture now known as the Harlem Renaissance. In addition to Fitzgerald and Armstrong, numerous musicians, including Duke Ellington, Fats Waller, and Bessie Smith, promoted their distinctive and complex music as an integral part of the emerging African American popular culture.

31. What is the main idea of the passage?

    a) People should associate jazz music with the 1920s, not modern New Orleans.

    b) Jazz music played an important role in many cultural movements of the 1920s.

    c) Many famous jazz musicians began their careers in New York City and Chicago.

    d) African Americans were instrumental in launching jazz into mainstream culture.

32. What can the reader conclude from the passage above?

    a) Jazz music was important to minority groups struggling for social equality in the 1920s.

    b) Duke Ellington, Fats Waller, and Bessie Smith were the most important jazz musicians of the Harlem Renaissance.

    c) Women were able to gain the right to vote with the help of jazz musicians.

    d) Duke Ellington, Fats Waller, and Bessie Smith all supported women's right to vote.

33. Which of the following is not a fact stated in the passage?

    a) The years between World War I and the Great Depression were known as the Jazz Age.

    b) Ella Fitzgerald and Louis Armstrong both moved to New York City to start their music careers.

    c) Women danced to jazz music during the 1920s to make a statement about their role in society.

    d) Jazz music was an integral part of the emerging African American popular culture of the 1920s.

34. What can the reader conclude from the passage above?

    a) F. Scott Fitzgerald supported jazz musicians in New York and Chicago.

    b) Jazz music is no longer as popular as it once was.

    c) Both women and African Americans used jazz music as a way of expressing their newfound freedom.

    d) Flappers and African American musicians worked together to produce jazz music.

35. What is the author's primary purpose in writing this essay?

    a) to explain the role jazz musicians played in the Harlem Renaissance

    b) to inform the reader about the many important musicians playing jazz in the 1920s

    c) to discuss how jazz influenced important cultural movements in the 1920s

    d) to provide a history of jazz music in the 20th century

36. Which of the following is the topic sentence for the whole passage?
   a) In recent decades, jazz has been associated with New Orleans and festivals like Mardi Gras, but in the 1920s jazz was a booming trend whose influence affected many aspects of American culture.
   b) Sometimes also called the Roaring Twenties, this time period saw major urban cities experiencing new economic, cultural, and artistic vitality.
   c) The Jazz Age brought along with it a more expressive and freed populace.
   d) Jazz music also provided the soundtrack for the explosion of African American art and culture now known as the Harlem Renaissance.

37. The passage is reflective of which of the following types of writing?
   a) technical
   b) expository
   c) persuasive
   d) narrative

38. Read the sentence below:
   Jazz music also provided the soundtrack for the explosion of African American art and culture now known as the Harlem Renaissance.
   This sentence appears in the second paragraph of the passage. This sentence is best described as which of the following?

   a) theme
   b) topic
   c) main idea
   d) supporting idea

Popcorn

Popcorn is often associated with fun and festivities, both in and out of the home. We eat it in theaters, smothering it in butter, and at home, fresh from the microwave. But popcorn isn't just for fun—it's also a multimillion-dollar industry with a long and fascinating history.

While popcorn might seem like a modern invention, its history actually dates back thousands of years, making it one of the oldest snack foods enjoyed around the world. Popping is believed by food historians to be one of the earliest uses of cultivated corn. In 1948, Herbert Dick and Earle Smith discovered old popcorn dating back 4000 years in the New Mexico Bat Cave. For the Aztecs who called the caves home, popcorn (or *momochitl)* played an important role in society, both as a food staple and in ceremonies. The Aztecs cooked popcorn by heating sand in a fire; when it was heated, kernels were added and would pop when exposed to the heat of the sand.

The American love affair with popcorn began in 1912, when it was first sold in theaters. The popcorn industry flourished during the Great Depression by advertising popcorn as a wholesome and economical food. Selling for five to ten cents a bag, it was a luxury that the downtrodden could afford. With the introduction of mobile popcorn machines at the World's Columbian Exposition, popcorn moved from the theater into fairs and parks.

Popcorn continued to rule the snack food kingdom until the rise in popularity of home televisions during the 1950s.

The popcorn industry quickly reacted to its decline in sales by introducing pre-popped and un-popped popcorn for home consumption. However, it wasn't until microwave popcorn became commercially available in 1981 that at-home popcorn consumption began to grow exponentially. With the wide availability of microwaves in the United States, popcorn also began popping up in offices and hotel rooms. The home still remains the most popular popcorn eating spot, though: today, seventy percent of the sixteen billion quarts of popcorn consumed annually in the United States is eaten at home.

39. What can the reader conclude from the passage above?
    a) People ate less popcorn in the 1950s than in previous decades because they went to the movies less.
    b) Without mobile popcorn machines, people would not have been able to eat popcorn during the Great Depression.
    c) People enjoyed popcorn during the Great Depression because it was a luxury food.
    d) During the 1800s, people began abandoning theaters to go to fairs and festivals.

40. What is the author's primary purpose in writing this essay?
    a) to explain how microwaves affected the popcorn industry
    b) to show that popcorn, while popular in American history, is older than many people realize
    c) to illustrate the global history of popcorn from ancient cultures to modern times
    d) to demonstrate the importance of popcorn in various cultures

Test Your Knowledge: Language Arts – The Reading Section – Answers

1. a)	21. c)
2. c)	22. c)
3. d)	23. d)
4. c)	24. a)
5. a)	25. d)
6. a)	26. b)
7. a)	27. c)
8. b)	28. b)
9. d)	29. a)
10. c)	30. a)
11. a)	31. b)
12. c)	32. a)
13. a)	33. b)
14. b)	34. c)
15. b)	35. c)
16. a)	36. a)
17. a)	37. b)
18. d)	38. c)
19. a)	39. a)
20. c)	40. b)

Chapter 2: Language

This section is divided into two parts: a series of multiple-choice questions which will test your knowledge of grammar, structure, and syntax. You will have 55 minutes to answer 55 questions.

Nouns, Pronouns, Verbs, Adjectives, and Adverbs

Nouns
Nouns are people, places, or things. They are typically the subject of a sentence. For example, "The hospital was very clean." The noun is "hospital;" it is the "place."

Pronouns
Pronouns essentially "replace" nouns. This allows a sentence to not sound repetitive. Take the sentence: "Sam stayed home from school because Sam was not feeling well." The word "Sam" appears twice in the same sentence. Instead, you can use a pronoun and say, "Sam stayed at home because *he* did not feel well." Sounds much better, right?

Most Common Pronouns:

- I, me, mine, my.

- You, your, yours.

- He, him, his.

- She, her, hers.

- It, its.

- We, us, our, ours.

- They, them, their, theirs.

Verbs
Remember the old commercial, "Verb: It's what you do"? That sums up verbs in a nutshell! Verbs are the "action" of a sentence; verbs "do" things.

They can, however, be quite tricky. Depending on the subject of a sentence, the tense of the word (past, present, future, etc.), and whether or not they are regular or irregular, verbs have many variations.

Example: "He runs to second base." The verb is "runs." This is a "regular verb."

Example: "I am 7 years old." The verb in this case is "am." This is an "irregular verb."

As mentioned, verbs must use the correct tense – and that tense must remain the same throughout the sentence. "I was baking cookies and eat some dough." That sounded strange, didn't it? That's because the two verbs "baking" and "eat" are presented in different tenses. "Was baking" occurred in the past; "eat," on the other hand, occurs in the present. Instead, it should be "**ate** some dough."

41

Adjectives

Adjectives are words that describe a noun and give more information. Take the sentence: "The boy hit the ball." If you want to know more about the noun "boy," then you could use an adjective to describe it. "The **little** boy hit the ball." An adjective simply provides more information about a noun or subject in a sentence.

Adverb

For some reason, many people have a difficult time with adverbs – but don't worry! They are really quite simple. Adverbs are similar to adjectives in that they provide more information about a part of a sentence; however, they do **not** describe nouns – that's an adjective's job. Instead, adverbs describe verbs, adjectives, and even other adverbs.

Take the sentence: "The doctor said she hired a new employee."

It would give more information to say: "The doctor said she **recently** hired a new employee." Now we know more about *how* the action was executed. Adverbs typically describe when or how something has happened, how it looks, how it feels, etc.

Good vs. Well

A very common mistake that people make concerning adverbs is the misuse of the word "good."

"Good" is an adjective – things taste good, look good, and smell good. "Good" can even be a noun – "Superman does good" – when the word is speaking about "good" vs. "evil." HOWEVER, "good" is never an adverb.

People commonly say things like, "I did really good on that test," or, "I'm good." Ugh! This is NOT the correct way to speak! In those sentences, the word "good" is being used to describe an action: how a person **did**, or how a person **is**. Therefore, the adverb "well" should be used. "I did really **well** on that test." "I'm **well**."

The correct use of "well" and "good" can make or break a person's impression of your grammar – make sure to always speak correctly!

Study Tips for Improving Vocabulary and Grammar

1. Visit the Online Writing Lab website, which is sponsored by Purdue University, at http://owl.english.purdue.edu. This site provides you with an excellent overview of syntax, writing style, and strategy. It also has helpful and lengthy review sections that include multiple-choice "Test Your Knowledge" quizzes, which provide immediate answers to the questions.

2. It's beneficial to read the entire passage first to determine its intended meaning BEFORE you attempt to answer any questions. Doing so provides you with key insight into a passage's syntax (especially verb tense, subject-verb agreement, modifier placement, writing style, and punctuation).

3. When you answer a question, eliminate incorrect answers to determine the best answer. Try each of the four answers and determine which one BEST fits with the meaning of the paragraph. Find the BEST answer. Chances are that the BEST answer is the CORRECT answer.

Practice Sentence Improvement

To give you a better idea of what you can expect from this section of the test, here are a few sample sentence improvement questions.

Paragraph A
Of the two types of eclipses, the most common is the lunar eclipse, which occurs when a full moon passes through Earth's shadow. (1) The disc-shaped moon slowly disappears completely or turns a coppery red color. (2) Solar and lunar eclipses both occur from time to time. (3)

Paragraph B
During a solar eclipse, the moon passes between the Earth and Sun. (4) As the moon moves into alignment, it blocks the light from the Sun creating an eerie darkness. (5) When the moon is perfectly in position, the Sun's light is visible as a ring, or corona, around the dark disc of the moon. (6) A lunar eclipse can be viewed from anywhere on the nighttime half of Earth, a solar eclipse can only be viewed from a zone that is only about 200 miles wide and covers about one-half of a percent of Earth's total area. (7)

1. Sentence 1: "Of the two types of eclipses, the most common is the lunar eclipse, which occurs when a full moon passes through Earth's shadow." Which of the following shows the best correction?
   a) Change "most" to "more."
   b) Change "occurs" to "occur."
   c) Change "which" to "that."
   d) Change "Earth's" to "Earths'."
   e) No correction is necessary.

2. Sentence 2: "The disc-shaped moon slowly disappears completely or turns a coppery red color." If you rewrote sentence 2, beginning with "The disc-shaped moon slowly turns a coppery red color," the next word should be:
   a) And.
   b) But.
   c) When.
   d) Because.
   e) Or.

3. How could paragraph A's effectiveness be improved?
   a) Move sentence 3 to the beginning of the paragraph.
   b) Remove sentence 2.
   c) Move sentence 2 to the beginning of the paragraph.
   d) Remove sentence 1.
   e) No revision is necessary.

4. Sentence 7: "A lunar eclipse can be viewed from anywhere on the nighttime half of <u>Earth, a solar eclipse</u> can only be viewed from a zone that is only about 200 miles wide and covers about one-half of a percent of Earth's total area." How could the underlined part of this sentence best be rewritten? If the original is the best way, choose option **a)**.
   a) "Earth, a solar eclipse"
   b) "Earth a solar eclipse"
   c) "Earth; a solar eclipse"
   d) "Earth, because a solar eclipse"
   e) "Earth, when a solar eclipse"

Answers:

1. **a)**
   Use the comparative "more" when comparing only two things. Here, you comparing two types of eclipses, so "more" is correct. The other changes introduce errors.

2. **e)**
   The clauses are joined by the conjunction "or" in the original sentence. Maintaining this conjunction maintains the original relationship between ideas.

3. **a)**
   As sentence 3 would serve as a good topic sentence, as well as an effective lead into sentence 1, the paragraph could be improved by moving sentence 3 to the beginning.

4. **c)**
   The two related sentences should be separated by a semicolon. The other answers introduce incorrect punctuation or an inaccurate relationship between the sentences.

Test Your Knowledge: Language Practice Test

Questions 1 – 5 are based on the following original passage. Sentences are numbered at the end for easy reference within the questions.

Examining the impact my lifestyle has on the earth's resources is, I believe, a fascinating and valuable thing to do (1). According to the Earth Day Network ecological footprint calculator, it would take four planet earths to sustain the human population if everyone used as many resources as I do (2). My "ecological footprint," or the amount of productive area of the earth that is required to produce the resources I consume, is therefore larger than the footprints of most of the population (3). It is hard to balance the luxuries and opportunities I have available to me with doing what I know to be better from an ecological standpoint (4).

It is fairly easy for me to recycle, so I do it, but it would be much harder to forgo the opportunity to travel by plane or eat my favorite fruits that have been flown to the supermarket from a different country (5). Although I get ecological points for my recycling habits, my use of public transportation, and living in an apartment complex rather than a free-standing residence, <u>my footprint expands when it is taken into account my not-entirely-local diet</u>, my occasional use of a car, my three magazine subscriptions, and my history of flying more than ten hours a year (6). I feel that realizing just how unfair my share of the earth's resources have been should help me to change at least some of my bad habits (7).

1. Which of the following shows the best version of sentence 1?
   a) It is fascinating and valuable to examine the impact that my lifestyle has on the earth's resources.
   b) Examining the impact my lifestyle has on the earth's resources is a fascinating and valuable thing to do.
   c) To examine the impact my lifestyle has on the earth's resources is fascinating and is also valuable.
   d) The impact of my lifestyle on the earth's resources is fascinating and valuable to examine.
   e) Examining the impact my lifestyle has on the earth's resources is, I believe, a fascinating and valuable thing to do.

2. Sentence 4 would best fit if it were moved where in this composition?
   a) At the beginning of paragraph 2.
   b) After sentence 5.
   c) After sentence 6.
   d) At the end of paragraph 2.
   e) Sentence 4 is best left where it is.

3. Which two sentences would be improved by switching positions?
   a) 1 and 2.
   b) 2 and 7.
   c) 3 and 4.
   d) 5 and 6.
   e) 6 and 7.

4. How could sentences 2 and 3 best be combined?
   a) According to the Earth Day Network ecological footprint calculator, it would take four planet earths to sustain the human population if everyone used as many resources as I do because I have a very large "ecological footprint," which is the amount of productive area of the earth that is required to produce the resources I consume.
   b) According to the Earth Day Network ecological footprint calculator, which calculates the amount of productive area of the earth that is required to produce the resources one consumes, it would take four planet earths to sustain the human population if everyone had a footprint as large as mine.
   c) According to the Earth Day Network ecological footprint calculator, it would take four planet earths to sustain the human population if everyone used as many resources as I do; my "ecological footprint," or the amount of productive area of the earth that is required to produce the resources I consume, is therefore larger than the footprints of most of the population.
   d) According to the Earth Day Network ecological footprint calculator, which measures the amount of productive area of the earth that is required to produce the resources a person consumes, my footprint is larger than that of most; it would take four planet earths to sustain the human population if everyone consumed as much as I do.
   e) According to the Earth Day Network ecological footprint calculator, my "ecological footprint," or the amount of productive area of the earth that is required to produce the resources I consume, would require four planet earths if it were to be the footprint of the human population; it is therefore larger than the footprints of most of the population.

5. How could the underlined part of sentence 6 best be rewritten?
   a) "my footprint expands when taken into account my not-entirely-local diet"
   b) "my footprint expands when taken into account are my not-entirely-local diet"
   c) "my footprint expands when we take into account my not-entirely-local diet"
   d) "my footprint expands when one takes into account my not-entirely-local diet"
   e) "my footprint expands when it is taken into account my not-entirely-local diet"

6. Which revision would most improve sentence 7?
   a) Eliminate the phrase "I feel that."
   b) Change "should help me" to "will help me."
   c) Add the phrase "In conclusion," to the beginning.
   d) Change "have been" to "has been."
   e) Eliminate the phrase "at least some of."

Questions 7 – 12 are based on the short passage below, which is excerpted from Thomas Huxley's preface to his Collected Essays: Volume V (public domain) and modified slightly. Sentences are numbered at the end for easy reference within the questions.

I had set out on a journey, with no other purpose than that of exploring a certain province of natural knowledge, I strayed no hair's breadth from the course which it was my right and my duty to pursue; and yet I found that, whatever route I took, before long, I came to a tall and formidable-looking fence (1). Confident I might be in the existence of an ancient and indefeasible right of way, before me stood the thorny barrier with its comminatory notice-board—"No Thoroughfare. By order" (2). There seemed no way over; nor did the prospect of creeping round, as I saw some do, attracts me (3). True there was no longer any cause to fear the spring guns and man-traps set by former lords of the manor; but one is apt to get very dirty going on all-fours (4). The only alternatives were either to give up my journey—which I was not minded to do—or to break the fence down and go through it (5). I swiftly ruled out crawling under as an option (6). I also ruled out turning back (7).

7. How could sentence 1 best be changed?
    a) The comma after journey should be removed.
    b) The comma after knowledge should be changed to a semicolon.
    c) "and yet" should be eliminated.
    d) Change "I had set out" to "I set out."
    e) No change.

8. Sentence 6 should be placed where in the passage?
    a) After sentence 1.
    b) After sentence 2.
    c) After sentence 3.
    d) After sentence 4.
    e) Left after sentence 5.

9. Which edit should be made in sentence 3?
    a) "nor" should be changed to "or."
    b) "seemed" should be changed to "seems."
    c) "me" should be changed to "I."
    d) "attracts" should be changed to "attract."
    e) No edit should be made.

10. How could sentences 6 and 7 best be combined?
    a) Swiftly, I ruled out crawling under as an option and also turning back.
    b) Ruling out two options swiftly: crawling under and turning back.
    c) I swiftly ruled out the options of crawling under or turning back.
    d) I ruled out crawling under as an option and I swiftly also ruled out turning back.
    e) I swiftly ruled out crawling under as an option and also turning back.

11. Which word could be inserted at the beginning of sentence 2 before "confident" to best clarify the meaning?
    a) Even.
    b) However.
    c) Hardly.
    d) Finally.
    e) Especially.

12. Which of the following is the best way to split sentence 1 into two separate sentences?

a) I had set out on a journey, with no other purpose than that of exploring a certain province of natural knowledge. I strayed no hair's breadth from the course which it was my right and my duty to pursue; and yet I found that, whatever route I took, before long, I came to a tall and formidable-looking fence.

b) I had set out on a journey, with no other purpose than that of exploring a certain province of natural knowledge, I strayed no hair's breadth from the course which it was my right and my duty to pursue. Yet I found that, whatever route I took, before long, I came to a tall and formidable-looking fence.

c) I had set out on a journey, with no other purpose than that of exploring a certain province of natural knowledge, I strayed no hair's breadth from the course which it was my right and my duty to pursue; and yet I found that, whatever route I took, before long. I came to a tall and formidable-looking fence.

d) I had set out on a journey. With no other purpose than that of exploring a certain province of natural knowledge, I strayed no hair's breadth from the course which it was my right and my duty to pursue; and yet I found that, whatever route I took, before long, I came to a tall and formidable-looking fence.

e) I had set out on a journey, with no other purpose than that of exploring a certain province of natural knowledge, I strayed no hair's breadth from the course which it was my right and my duty to pursue; and yet. I found that, whatever route I took, before long, I came to a tall and formidable-looking fence.

Questions 13 – 16 are based on the short passage below:

Who doesn't love a good cat meme? (1) It turns out that cats are more popular around the world than anyone had realized; with the proliferation of YouTube and social media, cats have taken the internet by storm. (2) From Grumpy Cat to Waffles, from the United States to Japan, cats appear in funny pictures, hilarious videos, and have even gone on to make their owners millions of dollars. (3)

Until recently, it had been believed that dogs were the most popular pet in the United States, with cats lagging behind in second place. (4) Dogs, "man's best friend," can be trained to do certain tricks and tasks, can be fun workout companions who play Frisbee and fetch with their owners, and can even help protect property. (5) While cats may have their uses in pest control, they are often reluctant to work on command, and very few are willing to submit to the humiliation of a collar and leash for a walk outside. (6) Still, it turns out that their funny antics and remarkable athletic prowess, even indoors, make for good TV.

(7) And so the internet is filled with cats large and small, lean and fat, wearing pieces of bread, making playthings out of boxes, jumping to amazing heights, and just looking hilariously grumpy. (8) Cats of internet fame now appear at conventions and festivals around the world, and people wait in line for hours just for a glimpse at their favorite feline celebrity. (9)

13. Which sentence best completes the first paragraph in order to create a good transition between two paragraphs?

    a) But cats have not always been in the spotlight; in fact, they had been relegated to a secondary position in the known hierarchy of pet popularity in popular culture.

    b) Indeed, cats are taking the world by storm.

    c) Cats are by far the most popular pet in the world, and cat ownership continues to rise.

    d) Thanks to the internet, cat marketability is becoming a field requiring true expertise, and there are even entrepreneurs who specialize in representing felines and their owners in public relations.

14. Which revision more concisely revises sentences (6) and (7)?

    a) No change

    b) On the other hand, cats are useful for pest control, they are often reluctant to work on command, and very few are willing to submit to the humiliation of a collar and leash for a walk outside. (6) However, it turns out that their funny antics and remarkable athletic prowess, even indoors, make for good TV. (7)

    c) Cats are useful for pest control, but they are often reluctant to work on command; moreover, very few are willing to submit to the humiliation of a collar and leash for a walk outside. (6) But it turns out that cats are more interesting—and funnier—than anyone realized, and their antics make for good TV. (7)

    d) Cats are funnier and more interesting than dogs, but are only good for pest control—they won't go for walks on leashes or learn commands.

15. What would be the best sentence to follow sentence 9, in keeping with the theme of the entire paragraph?

    a) Some dog owners are getting in on the act too, filming their dogs doing funny things and putting them on YouTube, but they don't get nearly as many hits as the cats do…at least not yet.

    b) Some of the cat owners have become quite media-savvy, and their cats now grace everything from coffee mugs to key chains to t-shirts; while waiting in line, fans are often enticed to buy these trinkets, but this irritates some fans.

    c) Some commentators believe that the cat owners are exploiting their cats, who no doubt would prefer to be at home napping in the sun or chasing mice.

    d) We mourn internet sensations like Chairman Meow who have passed on, and laud newcomers like Smushyface who have risen to the challenge of feline fame.

16. What would be a good title for this essay, keeping in mind both the topic and the tone?

    a) The Rise and Fall of Famous Felines: From Grumpy Cat to Smushyface

    b) Dog versus Cat: the Battle Continues, from the Internet to the Convention Center

    c) Felines Online! Pet Popularity, Feline Fame, and the Internet Age

    d) Cats for Cash: is Feline Fame Really Catsploitation?

Questions 17 – 20 are based on the passage below.

It sometimes seems like controversy over social media is never-ending. (1) Social media helps keep friends and family members in touch, helps transmit important news, from weather alerts to updates from warzones, out to the community and to the world, and provides opportunities for businesses to promote their products and reach new customers. (2) However, it also puts vulnerable people at risk, especially teenagers. (3) Cyber-bullying is on the rise, with sad stories of teenage depression and even suicide as a result of it appearing in the news. (4)

Vulnerable people can connect with people in similar difficult circumstances through Facebook groups, online forums, and other sources to find support. (5) Anonymous meeting points are especially helpful for people who are in recovery from mental illnesses like depression or eating disorders; they can confide in other people who have suffered from the same diseases and find the support they need. (6) Not everyone has access to counseling or the means to afford it; perhaps some forms of social media could be a stopgap solution for those in need. (7) Still, there is always the risk of "trolls," people who join these groups only to bully and shame people who really need help. (8)

17. Which sentence best completes the first paragraph in order to create a good transition between two paragraphs?
    a) Social media might do more harm than good in a cruel, unpredictable world; the anonymous world of the internet only brings out the worst in people, and we all must do our part to protect the most vulnerable.
    b) Many people argue that despite its uses, some restrictions should be placed on social media, especially the larger, more influential outlets like Facebook and Twitter.
    c) It might be said that social media is a two-edged sword, something that can enable supportive interaction but also risk facilitating hurtful, abusive behavior.
    d) The tragic stories of cyber-bullying only show that age limits should be placed on social media and even internet use; clearly, teenagers are unable to make good decisions when it comes to social situations, and the anonymity of the internet only enables abusive behavior.

18. What would be the best way to rewrite sentence 5?
    a) No change
    b) Many people who suffer from mental illnesses are isolated and vulnerable to cyber-bullying; social media can provide forums where they can find support from others in similar positions.
    c) It is hard for people who struggle with cyber-bullying because they might also suffer from mental illnesses and therefore feel very alone. With social media, they can connect with other people who also suffer from mental illnesses and form online support groups.
    d) Thanks to the anonymity of the internet, people can stay anonymous and still use social media to connect with other people and find support so they don't feel so alone.

19. What sentence would <u>best</u> follow sentence 8?

a) Unfortunately the internet is plagued by trolls; finding respite from bullies online even in safe zones set up for the vulnerable is nearly impossible, so members of such groups or sites must remain vigilant and enforce rules about what constitutes abusive behavior.

b) Fortunately, in these supportive environments, the bullied can become bullies themselves and drive the trolls away – a fate they deserve.

c) No one is sure how the word *trolls* came to describe online bullies, but it is surely a title they deserve; hiding behind anonymity in order to hurt other people's feelings is nothing to be proud of.

d) Thanks to online moderators, people may only join supportive online communities after a rigorous screening process, including background checks.

20. Read this sentence:

Some people feel very isolated or ashamed of mental illnesses or emotional conditions, to the point where they are not comfortable seeking out help, or do not know where to turn to get it; fears of criticism, being thought of as "crazy", losing friends, jobs, and other stigma may prevent them from pursuing therapy or treatment.

Where would this sentence <u>best</u> be placed in the draft essay?

a) after sentence 3

b) after sentence 7

c) before sentence 5

d) after sentence 5

Questions 21 – 24 are based on the passage below.

To stay or not to stay? (1) That is the question that faces many high school students as they consider colleges. (2) Whether to attend a college far from home depends on a variety of factors, from cost to personal preference, from opportunities at home to connections around the country or even around the world. (3)

Cost and family are two important factors. One student from Louisiana won a full scholarship to a school in California. (4) So even though she was admitted to several nearby schools in her home state, it was cheaper for her to move across the country, even though she would be far from her family. (5) Another student chose to stay home in Wisconsin and attend a state school for a year in order to save money on tuition and room and board; following his freshman year, he was able to apply to his out-of-state dream school in Chicago and could afford three years away from home. (6)

21. Which sentence best starts the second paragraph in order to create a good transition between two paragraphs?

    a) A recent study of several students across the nation revealed some of the reasons students chose to leave home or stay there for their college years.

    b) The sheer size of the United States provides limitless opportunities for young people seeking a university education; fifty states and six time zones gives students – even those without passports – a lot of options.

    c) Some states, like Texas and California, are so big in terms of geographic size and population that it is possible for a student to attend a great school without even leaving his or her home state.

    d) It can be hard for many students to leave their home region because of the many cultural differences found across our country, but it is a great learning experience for young people in the long term.

22. What would be the best example to use to develop the second paragraph?

    a) a student who travels from Florida to South America to learn Spanish for a year before attending university in Texas, in order to better prepare to major in Latin American studies

    b) a student from North Carolina who chooses to study in Arizona because her aunt and uncle live there; she is familiar with the state and can live with them for her first year of college

    c) a student from Maine who is considering college but plans to join the military after high school

    d) a student who wins a sports scholarship and so attends a university to play on its football team

23. What would be a good way to open a third paragraph of this essay?

    a) Surely, it is important for students to follow their dreams, even if they must ignore their families' wishes and go to college in another state.

    b) Other factors students took into account were their academic and professional interests, seeking out schools that specialized in their chosen career paths or that had the best facilities and professors in their fields.

    c) Some students were willing to stay at home and work, even if it meant waiting a year or two to begin their studies.

    d) A tiny minority of students believed it was more important to get married and have children than to go to college, but only a few respondents reported this belief.

24. Review sentence 5:

So even though she was admitted to several nearby schools in her home state, it was cheaper for her to move across the country, even though she would be far from her family. (5)

What would be the <u>best</u> way to rewrite this sentence?

    a) Even though she had a lot of opportunities in her home state because she could go to college there and live with her family, she went across the country because it was cheaper, since she had a scholarship.
    b) It was cheaper for her to move across the country, even though she was admitted to several nearby schools, and even though she would be far from home.
    c) Despite being accepted to several nearby schools, it was cheaper for her to move across the country.
    d) Despite her acceptance to several nearby schools, it was cheaper for her to move across the country.

Questions 25 – 28 are based on the passage below.

Americans continue to debate the merits of legalizing drugs. (1) Although many states have decriminalized the possession of marijuana, and some have outright legalized it altogether, still others retain harsh penalties for its consumption. (2) There are no easy answers here. (3)

In some states, citizens have agreed on a policy of allowing the use of marijuana for therapeutic purposes. (4) Medical marijuana is used to treat a variety of ailments, and can be obtained with a prescription. (5) It has helped many people suffering from serious afflictions, like cancer, with chronic pain and other conditions. (6) More research must be done in order to uncover any other uses for the drug in medicine. (7) Still, detractors from medical marijuana fear that any level of legal tolerance for the drug is unsafe. (8) Their fears are not entirely unfounded. (9) There is ample evidence to suggest that people who struggle with drug addiction began by abusing marijuana. (10) This may not be a risk for all users, though. (11)

25. Which sentence <u>best</u> replaces sentence 3 in order to provide more clarity and better transition between the two paragraphs?
    a) For many states, a solution lies somewhere in the middle.
    b) Legalizing the use of marijuana for some purposes has been a solution agreed upon in a number of states.
    c) Several states have found consensus by legalizing marijuana for a limited number of uses.
    d) For sure, outright legalization is not the solution at the federal level.
26. Which sentence would <u>best</u> open the second paragraph?
    a) One compromise has been to legalize marijuana for use in medicine and healing.
    b) Some doctors believe in medical marijuana.
    c) It has been proven that in small doses, marijuana can be medically beneficial.
    d) Not all Americans believe that marijuana should be legal for medical uses, but it is still used in medicine in some states.

27. Read this sentence:

More research must be done in order to uncover any other uses for the drug in medicine. (7)

What is the <u>best</u> way to rewrite it?

     a) However, more research must be done in order to determine whether there are further therapeutic uses for marijuana.

     b) In this case, it is clear that no further research is needed as to the efficacy of medical marijuana, and research would be better spent on cures to these diseases.

     c) It is possible that it may have other uses in medicine as well; further research may lead to more information.

     d) Without further research, there would be no need to prescribe medical marijuana.

Questions 28-40 are based on the short passage below:

Traveling on commercial airlines has changed substantially <u>over years</u>. (1) When commercial air travel first became available, it was so expensive that usually only businessmen could afford <u>to do so</u>. (2) Airplane efficiency, the relative cost of fossil fuels, <u>and using economies</u> of scale have all contributed to make travel by air more affordable and common. (3) These days, there are nearly 30,000 commercial air flights in the world each day! (4)

Depending on the size of the airport you are departing from, you should arrive 90 minutes to two and a half hours before your plane leaves. (5) Things like checking your luggage and flying internationally can make the process of getting to your gate take longer. (6) If you fly out of a very busy airport, like <u>LaGuardia, in</u> New York City, on a very busy travel day, like the day before Thanksgiving, you can easily miss your flight if you don't arrive early enough. (7)

Security processes for passengers have also changed. (8) In the 1960s, there was <u>hardly any</u> security: you could just buy your ticket and walk on to the plane the day of the flight without even needing to show identification. (9) In the 1970s, American commercial airlines started installing sky marshals on many <u>flights, an</u> undercover law enforcement officers who would protect the passengers from a potential hijacking. (10)

Also in the early 1970s, the federal government began to require that airlines screen passengers and their luggage for things like weapons and bombs. (11) After the 2001 terrorist attacks in the United States, these requirements were <u>stringently enforced</u>. (12) Family members can no longer meet someone at the gate; <u>only ticketed passengers are allowed into the gate area</u>. (13) The definition of <u>weapons are</u> not allowed is expanded every time there is a new incident for example liquids are now restricted on planes after an attempted planned attack using gel explosives in 2006. (14)

Despite the hassles of traveling by air, it is still a boon to modern <u>life. (15) Still, some</u> businesses are moving away from sending employees on airplane trips, <u>as</u> face-to-face video conferencing technologies improve. (16) A trip which might take ten hours by car <u>can take only</u> two hours by plane. (17) However, the ability to travel quickly by air <u>will always be valued, by citizens</u> of our modern society. (18)

28. Which of the following is the best change to the underlined portion of sentence 1?
   a. No Change.
   b. "over the years"
   c. "over time"
   d. Delete.

29. Which of the following is the best change to the underlined portion of sentence 2?
   a. No Change.
   b. "to do it"
   c. "to fly"
   d. "do so"

30. Which of the following is the best change to the underlined portion of sentence 3?
   a. No Change.
   b. "using economies"
   c. "and the use of economies"
   d. "and economies"

31. Which of the following is the best change to the underlined portion of sentence 7?
   a. No Change.
   b. "La Guardia in"
   c. "La Guardia; in"
   d. "La Guardia,"

32. Which of the following is the best change to the underlined portion of sentence 9?
   a. No Change.
   b. "hardly"
   c. "no"
   d. "barely"

33. Which of the following is the best change to the underlined portion of sentence 10?
   a. No Change.
   b. "flights; an"
   c. "flights. Marshals are"
   d. "flights, marshals are"

34. Which of the following is the best change to the underlined portion of sentence 12?
   a. No Change.
   b. "stiffly upheld"
   c. "enforced with more stringency"
   d. "more stringently enforced"

35. If the underlined portion in sentence 13 were deleted, the passage would lose:
   a. No Change.
   b. An explanation of the screening process.
   c. Ambiguity over why family members are no longer allowed at the gate.
   d. A further specific example of how regulations have changed over time.

36. Which of the following is the best change to the underlined portion in sentence 14?

    a. No Change.
    b. "weapon is"
    c. "weapons"
    d. "weapons which are"

37. Which of the following is the proper transition between sentences 15 & 16?
    a. No Change.
    b. "life. Some"
    c. "life even though some"
    d. "life, still some"

38. Which of the following is the best replacement for the underlined word in sentence 16?
    a. No Change.
    b. "because"
    c. "while"
    d. "since"

39. Which of the following is the best change to the underlined portion in sentence 17?
    a. No Change.
    b. "may only take"
    c. "takes only"
    d. "will only take"

40. Which of the following is the best change to the underlined portion in sentence 18?
    a. No Change.
    b. "citizens will always value"
    c. "will always, be valued by citizens"
    d. "will always be valued by citizens"

Test Your Knowledge: Language – Answers

1. a).		25. b).	
2. c).		26. b).	
3. d).		27. b).	
4. d).		28. b).	
5. d).		29. c).	
6. d).		30. c).	
7. b).		31. b).	
8. d).		32. a).	
9. d).		33. c).	
10. c).		34. d).	
11. b).		35. d).	
12. a).		36. d).	
13. a).		37. c).	
14. c).		38. a).	
15. d).		39. b).	
16. c).		40. d).	
17. c).			
18. b).			
19. a).			
20. d).			
21. a).			
22. b).			
23. b).			
24. a).			

Chapter 3: Mathematics

The Most Common Mistakes

People make little mistakes all the time, but during a test those tiny mistakes can make the difference between a good score and a poor one. Watch out for these common mistakes that people make on the math section of the TABE:

- answering with the wrong sign (positive/negative)

- mixing up the order of operations

- misplacing a decimal

- not reading the question thoroughly (and therefore providing an answer that was not asked for)

- circling the wrong letter or filling in wrong circle choice

If you're thinking, *those ideas are just common sense*, that's exactly the point. Most of the mistakes made on the TABE are simple ones. But no matter how silly the mistake, a wrong answer still means a lost point on the test.

Strategies for the Mathematics Section

Go Back to the Basics

First and foremost, practice your basic skills: sign changes, order of operations, simplifying fractions, and equation manipulation. These are the skills used most on the TABE, though they are applied in different contexts. Remember that when it comes down to it, all math problems rely on the four basic skills of addition, subtraction, multiplication, and division. All you need to figure out is the order in which they're used to solve a problem.

Don't Rely on Mental Math

Using mental math is great for eliminating answer choices, but ALWAYS WRITE DOWN YOUR WORK! This cannot be stressed enough. Use whatever paper is provided; by writing and/or drawing out the problem, you are more likely to catch any mistakes. The act of writing things down also forces you to organize your calculations, leading to an improvement in your TABE score.

The Three-Times Rule

You should read each question at least three times to ensure you're using the correct information and answering the right question:

Step one: Read the question and write out the given information.

Step two: Read the question, set up your equation(s), and solve.

Step three: Read the question and check that your answer makes sense (is the amount too large or small; is the answer in the correct unit of measure, etc.).

Make an Educated Guess

Eliminate those answer choices which you are relatively sure are incorrect, and then guess from the remaining choices. Educated guessing is critical to increasing your score.

Numbers and Operations
Positive and Negative Number Rules

Adding, multiplying, and dividing numbers can yield positive or negative values depending on the signs of the original numbers. Knowing these rules can help determine if your answer is correct.

$(+) + (-)$ = the sign of the larger number

$(-) + (-)$ = negative number

$(-) \times (-)$ = positive number

$(-) \times (+)$ = negative number

$(-) \div (-)$ = positive number

$(-) \div (+)$ = negative number

Examples

1.   Find the product of -10 and 47.

$(-) \times (+) = (-)$

$-10 \times 47 = \mathbf{-470}$

2.   What is the sum of -65 and -32?

$(-) + (-) = (-)$

$-65 + -32 = \mathbf{-97}$

3.   Is the product of -7 and 4 less than -7, between -7 and 4, or greater than 4?

$(-) \times (+) = (-)$

$-7 \times 4 = -28$, which is **less than -7**

4.   What is the value of −16 divided by 2.5?

$(-) \div (+) = (-)$

$-16 \div 2.5 = \mathbf{-6.4}$

Order of Operations

Operations in a mathematical expression are always performed in a specific order, which is described by the acronym PEMDAS:

      1.   Parentheses

      2.   Exponents

      3.   Multiplication

      4.   Division

      5.   Addition

      6.   Subtraction

Perform the operations within parentheses first, and then address any exponents. After those steps, perform all multiplication and division. These are carried out from left to right as they appear in the problem.

Finally, do all required addition and subtraction, also from left to right as each operation appears in the problem.

Examples

1.   Solve: $[-(2)^2 - (4 + 7)]$

First, complete operations within parentheses:

$-(2)^2 - (11)$

Second, calculate the value of exponential numbers:

$-(4) - (11)$

Finally, do addition and subtraction:

$-4 - 11 = \mathbf{-15}$

2.   Solve: $(5)^2 \div 5 + 4 \times 2$

First, calculate the value of exponential numbers:

$(25) \div 5 + 4 \times 2$

Second, calculate division and multiplication from left to right:

$5 + 8$

Finally, do addition and subtraction:

$5 + 8 = \mathbf{13}$

3.   Solve the expression: $15 \times (4 + 8) - 3^3$

First, complete operations within parentheses:

$15 \times (12) - 3^3$

Second, calculate the value of exponential numbers:

$15 \times (12) - 27$

Third, calculate division and multiplication from left to right:

$180 - 27$

Finally, do addition and subtraction from left to right:

$180 - 27 = \mathbf{153}$

4.   Solve the expression: $(\frac{5}{2} \times 4) + 23 - 4^2$

First, complete operations within parentheses:

$(10) + 23 - 4^2$

Second, calculate the value of exponential numbers:

$(10) + 23 - 16$

Finally, do addition and subtraction from left to right:

$(10) + 23 - 16$

$33 - 16 = \mathbf{17}$

Greatest Common Factor

The greatest common factor (GCF) of a set of numbers is the largest number that can evenly divide into all of the numbers in the set. To find the GCF of a set, find all of the factors of each number in the set. A factor is a whole number that can be multiplied by another whole number to result in the original number. For example, the number 10 has four factors: 1, 2, 5, and 10. (When listing the factors of a number, remember to include 1 and the number itself.) The largest number that is a factor for each number in the set is the GCF.

Examples

1.   Find the greatest common factor of 24 and 18.

Factors of 24: 1, 2, 3, 4, 6, 8, 12, 24

Factors of 18: 1, 2, 3, 6, 9, 18

The greatest common factor is 6.

2.   Find the greatest common factor of 121 and 44.

Since these numbers are larger, it's easier to start with the smaller number when listing factors.

Factors of 44: 1, 2, 4, 11, 22, 44

Now, it's not necessary to list all of the factors of 121. Instead, we can eliminate those factors of 44 which do not divide evenly into 121:

121 is not evenly divisible by 2, 4, 22, or 44 because it is an odd number. This leaves only 1 and 11 as common factors, so the **GCF is 11**.

3.   First aid kits are being assembled at a summer camp. A complete first aid kit requires bandages, sutures, and sterilizing swabs, and each of the kits must be identical to other kits. If the camp's total supplies include 52 bandages, 13 sutures, and 39 sterilizing swabs, how many complete first aid kits can be assembled without having any leftover materials?

This problem is asking for the greatest common factor of 52, 13, and 39. The first step is to find all of the factors of the smallest number, 13.

Factors of 13: 1, 13

13 is a prime number, meaning that its only factors are 1 and itself. Next, we check to see if 13 is also a factor of 39 and 52:

$13 \times 2 = 26$

$13 \times 3 = 39$

$13 \times 4 = 52$

We can see that 39 and 52 are both multiples of 13. This means that **13 first aid kits can be made without having any leftover materials.**

4.   Elena is making sundaes for her friends. She has 20 scoops of chocolate ice cream and 16 scoops of strawberry. If she wants to make identical sundaes and use all of her ice cream, how many sundaes can she make?

Arranging things into identical groups with no leftovers is always a tip that the problem calls for finding the greatest common factor. To find the GCF of 16 and 20, the first step is to factor both numbers:

Factors of 16: 1, 2, 4, 8, 16

Factors of 20: 1, 2, 4, 5, 10, 20

From these lists, we see that **4 is the GCF**. Elena can make 4 sundaes, each with 5 scoops of chocolate ice cream and 4 scoops of strawberry. Any other combination would result in leftover ice cream or sundaes that are not identical.

Comparison of Rational Numbers

Number comparison problems present numbers in different formats and ask which is larger or smaller, or whether the numbers are equivalent. The important step in solving these problems is to convert the numbers to the same format so that it is easier to see how they compare. If numbers are given in the same format, or after they have been converted, determine which number is smaller or if the numbers are equal. Remember that for negative numbers, higher numbers are actually smaller.

Examples

1.   Is $4\frac{3}{4}$ greater than, equal to, or less than $\frac{18}{4}$?

These numbers are in different formats—one is a mixed fraction and the other is just a fraction. So, the first step is to convert the mixed fraction to a fraction:

$4\frac{3}{4} = \frac{4 \times 4 + 3}{4} = \frac{19}{4}$

Once the mixed number is converted, it is easier to see that $\frac{19}{4}$ is greater than $\frac{18}{4}$.

2.   Which of the following numbers has the greatest value: 104.56, 104.5, or 104.6?

These numbers are already in the same format, so the decimal values just need to be compared. Remember that zeros can be added after the decimal without changing the value, so the three numbers can be rewritten as:

104.56

104.50

104.60

From this list, it is clearer to see that **104.60 is the greatest** because 0.60 is larger than 0.50 and 0.56.

3.   Is 65% greater than, less than, or equal to $\frac{13}{20}$?

The first step is to convert the numbers into the same format. 65% is the same as $\frac{65}{100}$.

Next, the fractions need to be converted to have the same denominator. It is difficult to compare fractions with different denominators. Using a factor of $\frac{5}{5}$ on the second fraction will give common denominators:

$$\frac{13}{20} \times \frac{5}{5} = \frac{65}{100}$$

Now, it is easy to see that **the numbers are equivalent**.

Units of Measurement

You are expected to memorize some units of measurement. These are given below. When doing unit conversion problems (i.e., when converting one unit to another), find the conversion factor, then apply that factor to the given measurement to find the new units.

UNIT PREFIXES		
Prefix	**Symbol**	**Multiplication Factor**
tera	T	1,000,000,000,000
giga	G	1,000,000,000
mega	M	1,000,000
kilo	k	1,000
hecto	h	100

deca	da	10
base unit	--	--
deci	d	0.1
centi	c	0.01
milli	m	0.001
micro	μ	0.0000001
nano	n	0.0000000001
pico	p	0.0000000000001

UNITS AND CONVERSION FACTORS

Dimension	American	SI
length	inch/foot/yard/mile	meter
mass	ounce/pound/ton	gram
volume	cup/pint/quart/gallon	liter
force	pound-force	newton
pressure	pound-force per square inch	pascal
work and energy	cal/British thermal unit	joule
temperature	Fahrenheit	kelvin
charge	faraday	coulomb
Conversion Factors		

1 in. = 2.54 cm	1 lb. = 0.454 kg
1 yd. = 0.914 m	1 cal = 4.19 J
1 mi. = 1.61 km	$1°F = \frac{5}{9}(°F - 32°C)$
1 gal. = 3.785 L	$1 cm^3 = 1$ mL
1 oz. = 28.35 g	1 hr = 3600 s

Examples

1. A fence measures 15 ft. long. How many yards long is the fence?

1 yd. = 3 ft.

$\frac{15}{3}$ = **5 yd.**

2. A pitcher can hold 24 cups. How many gallons can it hold?

1 gal. = 16 cups

$\frac{24}{16}$ = **1.5 gallons**

3. A spool of wire holds 144 in. of wire. If Mario has 3 spools, how many feet of wire does he have?

12 in. = 1 ft.

$\frac{144}{12}$ = 12 ft.

12 ft. × 3 spools = **36 ft. of wire**

4. A ball rolling across a table travels 6 inches per second. How many feet will it travel in 1 minute?

This problem can be worked in two steps: finding how many inches are covered in 1 minute, and then converting that value to feet. It can also be worked the opposite way, by finding how many feet it travels in 1 second and then converting that to feet traveled per minute. The first method is shown below.

1 min. = 60 sec.

(6 in.)/(sec.) × 60 s = 360 in.

1 ft. = 12 in.

(360 in.)/(12 in.) = **30 ft.**

5. How many millimeters are in 0.5 m?

1 meter = 1000 mm

0.5 meters = **500 mm**

6. A lead ball weighs 38 g. How many kilograms does it weigh?

1 kg = 1000 g

$\frac{38}{1000}$ g = **0.038 kg**

7. How many cubic centimeters are in 10 L?

1 L = 1000 ml

10 L = 1000 ml × 10

10 L = **10,000 ml or cm³**

8. Jennifer's pencil was initially 10 centimeters long. After she sharpened it, it was 9.6 centimeters long. How many millimeters did she lose from her pencil by sharpening it?

1 cm = 10 mm

10 cm − 9.6 cm = 0.4 cm lost

0.4 cm = 10 × .4 mm = **4 mm were lost**

Decimals and Fractions

Adding and Subtracting Decimals
When adding and subtracting decimals, line up the numbers so that the decimals are aligned. You want to subtract the ones place from the ones place, the tenths place from the tenths place, etc.

Examples

1. Find the sum of 17.07 and 2.52.

17.07

+2.52

19.59

2. Jeannette has 7.4 gallons of gas in her tank. After driving, she has 6.8 gallons. How many gallons of gas did she use?

$$\begin{array}{r} 7.4 \\ -\ 6.8 \\ \hline 0.6 \text{ gal} \end{array}$$

Multiplying and Dividing Decimals

When multiplying decimals, start by multiplying the numbers normally. You can then determine the placement of the decimal point in the result by adding the number of digits after the decimal in each of the numbers you multiplied together.

When dividing decimals, you should move the decimal point in the divisor (the number you're dividing by) until it is a whole. You can then move the decimal in the dividend (the number you're dividing into) the same number of places in the same direction. Finally, divide the new numbers normally to get the correct answer.

Examples

1. What is the product of 0.25 and 1.4?

$25 \times 14 = 350$

There are 2 digits after the decimal in 0.25 and one digit after the decimal in 1.4. Therefore the product should have 3 digits after the decimal: **0.350** is the correct answer.

2. Find $0.8 \div 0.2$.

Change 0.2 to 2 by moving the decimal one space to the right.

Next, move the decimal one space to the right on the dividend. 0.8 becomes 8.

Now, divide 8 by 2. $8 \div 2 = \mathbf{4}$

3. Find the quotient when 40 is divided by 0.25.

First, change the divisor to a whole number: 0.25 becomes 25.

Next, change the dividend to match the divisor by moving the decimal two spaces to the right, so 40 becomes 4000.

Now divide: $4000 \div 25 = \mathbf{160}$

Working with Fractions

FRACTIONS are made up of two parts: the **NUMERATOR**, which appears above the bar, and the **DENOMINATOR**, which is below it. If a fraction is in its **SIMPLEST FORM**, the numerator and the denominator share no common factors. A fraction with a numerator larger than its denominator is an **IMPROPER FRACTION**; when the denominator is larger, it's a **PROPER FRACTION**.

Improper fractions can be converted into proper fractions by dividing the numerator by the denominator. The resulting whole number is placed to the left of the fraction, and the remainder becomes the new numerator; the denominator does not change. The new number is called a **MIXED NUMBER** because it contains a whole number and a fraction. Mixed numbers can be turned into improper fractions through the reverse process: multiply the whole number by the denominator and add the numerator to get the new numerator.

Examples

1. Simplify the fraction $\frac{121}{77}$.

121 and 77 share a common factor of 11. So, if we divide each by 11 we can simplify the fraction:

$$\frac{121}{77} = \frac{11}{11} \times \frac{11}{7} = \frac{11}{7}$$

2. Convert $\frac{37}{5}$ into a proper fraction.

Start by dividing the numerator by the denominator:

$37 \div 5 = 7$ with a remainder of 2

Now build a mixed number with the whole number and the new numerator:

$$\frac{37}{5} = 7\frac{2}{5}$$

Multiplying and Dividing Fractions

To multiply fractions, convert any mixed numbers into improper fractions and multiply the numerators together and the denominators together. Reduce to lowest terms if needed.

To divide fractions, first convert any mixed fractions into single fractions. Then, invert the second fraction so that the denominator and numerator are switched. Finally, multiply the numerators together and the denominators together.

Examples

1. What is the product of $\frac{1}{12}$ and $\frac{6}{8}$?

Simply multiply the numerators together and the denominators together, then reduce:

$$\frac{1}{12} \times \frac{6}{8} = \frac{6}{96} = \frac{1}{16}$$

Sometimes it's easier to reduce fractions before multiplying if you can:

$$\frac{1}{12} \times \frac{6}{8} = \frac{1}{12} \times \frac{3}{4} = \frac{3}{48} = \frac{1}{16}$$

2. Find $\frac{7}{8} \div \frac{1}{4}$.

For a fraction division problem, invert the second fraction and then multiply and reduce:

$$\frac{7}{8} \div \frac{1}{4} = \frac{7}{8} \times \frac{4}{1} = \frac{28}{8} = \frac{7}{2}$$

3. What is the quotient of $\frac{2}{5} \div 1\frac{1}{5}$?

This is a fraction division problem, so the first step is to convert the mixed number to an improper fraction:

$$1\frac{1}{5} = \frac{5 \times 1 + 1}{5} = \frac{6}{5}$$

Now, divide the fractions. Remember to invert the second fraction, and then multiply normally:

$$\frac{2}{5} \div \frac{6}{5} = \frac{2}{5} \times \frac{5}{6} = \frac{10}{30} = \frac{1}{3}$$

4. A recipe calls for $\frac{1}{4}$ cup of sugar. If 8.5 batches of the recipe are needed, how many cups of sugar will be used?

This is a fraction multiplication problem: $\frac{1}{4} \times 8\frac{1}{2}$.

First, we need to convert the mixed number into a proper fraction:

$$8\frac{1}{2} = \frac{8 \times 2 + 1}{2} = \frac{17}{2}$$

Now, multiply the fractions across the numerators and denominators, and then reduce:

$$\frac{1}{4} \times 8\frac{1}{2} = \frac{1}{4} \times \frac{17}{2} = \frac{17}{8} \text{ cups of sugar}$$

Adding and Subtracting Fractions

Adding and subtracting fractions requires a **COMMON DENOMINATOR**. To find the common denominator, you can multiply each fraction by the number 1. With fractions, any number over itself (e.g., $\frac{5}{5}$, $\frac{12}{12}$, etc.) is equivalent to 1, so multiplying by such a fraction can change the denominator without changing the value of the fraction. Once the denominators are the same, the numerators can be added or subtracted.

To add mixed numbers, you can first add the whole numbers and then the fractions. To subtract mixed numbers, convert each number to an improper fraction, then subtract the numerators.

Examples

1.   Simplify the expression $\frac{2}{3} - \frac{1}{5}$.

First, multiply each fraction by a factor of 1 to get a common denominator. How do you know which factor of 1 to use? Look at the other fraction and use the number found in that denominator:

$$\frac{2}{3} - \frac{1}{5} = \frac{2}{3}\left(\frac{5}{5}\right) - \frac{1}{5}\left(\frac{3}{3}\right) = \frac{10}{15} - \frac{3}{15}$$

Once the fractions have a common denominator, simply subtract the numerators:

$$\frac{10}{15} - \frac{3}{15} = \frac{7}{15}$$

2.   Find $2\frac{1}{3} - \frac{3}{2}$.

This is a fraction subtraction problem with a mixed number, so the first step is to convert the mixed number to an improper fraction:

$$2\frac{1}{3} = \frac{2 \times 3 + 1}{3} = \frac{7}{3}$$

Next, convert each fraction so they share a common denominator:

$$\frac{7}{3} \times \frac{2}{2} = \frac{14}{6}$$

$$\frac{3}{2} \times \frac{3}{3} = \frac{9}{6}$$

Now, subtract the fractions by subtracting the numerators:

$$\frac{14}{6} - \frac{9}{6} = \frac{5}{6}$$

3.   Find the sum of $\frac{9}{16}, \frac{1}{2}$, and $\frac{7}{4}$.

For this fraction addition problem, we need to find a common denominator. Notice that 2 and 4 are both factors of 16, so 16 can be the common denominator:

$$\frac{1}{2} \times \frac{8}{8} = \frac{8}{16}$$

$$\frac{7}{4} \times \frac{4}{4} = \frac{28}{16}$$

$$\frac{9}{16} + \frac{8}{16} + \frac{28}{16} = \frac{45}{16}$$

4.   Sabrina has $\frac{2}{3}$ of a can of red paint. Her friend Amos has $\frac{1}{6}$ of a can. How much red paint do they have combined?

To add fractions, make sure that they have a common denominator. Since 3 is a factor of 6, 6 can be the common denominator:

$$\frac{2}{3} \times \frac{2}{2} = \frac{4}{6}$$

Now, add the numerators:

$$\frac{4}{6} + \frac{1}{6} = \frac{5}{6} \text{ of a can}$$

Converting Fractions to Decimals

Calculators are not allowed on the TABE, which can make handling fractions and decimals intimidating for many test takers. However, there are several techniques you can use to help you convert between the two forms.

The first thing to do is simply memorize common decimals and their fractional equivalents; a list of these is given in Table 3.4. With these values, it's possible to convert more complicated fractions as well. For example, $\frac{2}{5}$ is just $\frac{1}{5}$ multiplied by 2, so $\frac{2}{5} = 0.2 \times 2 = 0.4$.

COMMON DECIMALS AND FRACTIONS	
fraction	decimal
$\frac{1}{2}$	0.5
$\frac{1}{3}$	$0.\overline{33}$
$\frac{1}{4}$	0.25
$\frac{1}{5}$	0.2
$\frac{1}{6}$	$0.1\overline{66}$
$\frac{1}{7}$	$0.\overline{142857}$
$\frac{1}{8}$	0.125
$\frac{1}{9}$	$0.\overline{11}$
$\frac{1}{10}$	0.1

Knowledge of common decimal equivalents to fractions can also help you estimate. This skill can be particularly helpful on multiple-choice tests like the TABE, where excluding incorrect answers can be just as helpful as knowing how to find the right one. For example, to find $\frac{5}{8}$ in decimal form for an answer, you can eliminate any answers less than 0.5 because $\frac{4}{8} = 0.5$. You may also know that $\frac{6}{8}$ is the same as $\frac{3}{4}$ or 0.75, so anything above 0.75 can be eliminated as well.

Another helpful trick can be used if the denominator is easily divisible by 100: in the fraction $\frac{9}{20}$, you know 20 goes into 100 five times, so you can multiply the top and bottom by 5 to get $\frac{45}{100}$ or 0.45.

If none of these techniques work, you'll need to find the decimal by dividing the denominator by the numerator using long division.

Examples

1.   Write $\frac{8}{18}$ as a decimal.

The first step here is to simplify the fraction:

$$\frac{8}{18} = \frac{4}{9}$$

Now it's clear that the fraction is a multiple of $\frac{1}{9}$, so you can easily find the decimal using a value you already know:

$$\frac{4}{9} = \frac{1}{9} \times 4 = 0.\overline{11} \times 4 = \mathbf{0.\overline{44}}$$

2.   Write the fraction $\frac{3}{16}$ as a decimal.

None of the tricks above will work for this fraction, so you need to do long division:

The decimal will go in front of the answer, so now you know that $\frac{3}{16} = \mathbf{0.1875}$.

Converting Decimals to Fractions

Converting a decimal into a fraction is more straightforward than the reverse process is. To convert a decimal, simply use the numbers that come after the decimal as the numerator in the fraction. The denominator will be a power of 10 that matches the place value for the original decimal. For example, the numerator for 0.46 would be 100 because the last number is in the tenths place; likewise, the denominator for 0.657 would be 1000 because the last number is in the thousandths place. Once this fraction has been set up, all that's left is to simplify it.

Example

Convert 0.45 into a fraction.

The last number in the decimal is in the hundredths place, so we can easily set up a fraction:

$$0.45 = \frac{45}{100}$$

The next step is to simply reduce the fraction down to the lowest common denominator. Here, both 45 and 100 are divisible by 5: 45 divided by 5 is 9, and 100 divided by 5 is 20. Therefore, you're left with:

$$\frac{45}{100} = \frac{9}{20}$$

Ratios

A **RATIO** tells you how many of one thing exists in relation to the number of another thing. Unlike fractions, ratios do not give a part relative to a whole; instead, they compare two values. For example, if you have 3 apples and 4 oranges, the ratio of apples to oranges is 3 to 4. Ratios can be written using words (3 to 4), fractions $\left(\frac{3}{4}\right)$, or colons (3:4).

In order to work with ratios, it's helpful to rewrite them as a fraction expressing a part to a whole. For example, in the example above you have 7 total pieces of fruit, so the fraction of your fruit that are apples is $\frac{3}{7}$, and oranges make up $\frac{4}{7}$ of your fruit collection.

One last important thing to consider when working with ratios is the units of the values being compared. On the TABE, you may be asked to rewrite a ratio using the same units on both sides. For example, you might have to rewrite the ratio 3 minutes to 7 seconds as 180 seconds to 7 seconds.

Examples

1.   There are 90 voters in a room, and each is either a Democrat or a Republican. The ratio of Democrats to Republicans is 5:4. How many Republicans are there?

We know that there are 5 Democrats for every 4 Republicans in the room, which means for every 9 people, 4 are Republicans.

$5 + 4 = 9$

Fraction of Democrats: $\frac{5}{9}$

Fraction of Republicans: $\frac{4}{9}$

If $\frac{4}{9}$ of the 90 voters are Republicans, then:

$\frac{4}{9} \times 90 =$ **40 voters are Republicans**

2. The ratio of students to teachers in a school is 15:1. If there are 38 teachers, how many students attend the school?

To solve this ratio problem, we can simply multiply both sides of the ratio by the desired value to find the number of students that correspond to having 38 teachers:

$$\frac{15 \text{ students}}{1 \text{ teacher}} \times 38 \text{ teachers} = 570 \text{ students}$$

The school has **570 students**.

Proportions

A **PROPORTION** is an equation which states that 2 ratios are equal. Proportions are usually written as 2 fractions joined by an equal sign $\left(\frac{a}{b} = \frac{c}{d}\right)$, but they can also be written using colons ($a : b :: c : d$). Note that in a proportion, the units must be the same in both numerators and in both denominators.

Often you will be given 3 of the values in a proportion and asked to find the 4th. In these types of problems, you can solve for the missing variable by cross-multiplying—multiply the numerator of each fraction by the denominator of the other to get an equation with no fractions as shown below. You can then solve the equation using basic algebra. (For more on solving basic equations, see *Algebraic Expressions and Equations*.)

$$\frac{a}{b} = \frac{c}{d} \rightarrow ad = bc$$

Examples

1. A train traveling 120 miles takes 3 hours to get to its destination. How long will it take for the train to travel 180 miles?

Start by setting up the proportion:

$$\frac{120 \text{ miles}}{3 \text{ hours}} = \frac{180 \text{ miles}}{x \text{ hours}}$$

Note that it doesn't matter which value is placed in the numerator or denominator, as long as it is the same on both sides. Now, solve for the missing quantity through cross–multiplication:

$$120 \text{ miles} \times x \text{ hours} = 3 \text{ hours} \times 180 \text{ miles}$$

Now solve the equation:

$$x = \frac{3 \text{ hours} \times 180 \text{ miles}}{120 \text{ miles}}$$

x = **4.5 hours**

2.   One acre of wheat requires 500 gallons of water. How many acres can be watered with 2600 gallons?

Set up the equation:

$$\frac{1 \text{ acre}}{500 \text{ gal.}} = \frac{x \text{ acres}}{2600 \text{ gal.}}$$

Then solve for x:

$$x = \frac{1 \text{ acre} \times 2600 \text{ gal.}}{500 \text{ gal.}}$$

$x = \frac{26}{5}$ or **5.2 acres**

3.   If $35 : 5 :: 49 : x$, find x.

This problem presents two equivalent ratios that can be set up in a fraction equation:

$$\frac{35}{5} = \frac{49}{x}$$

You can then cross-multiply to solve for x:

$$35x = 49 \times 5$$

$$x = 7$$

Percentages

A **PERCENT** is the ratio of a part to the whole. Questions may give the part and the whole and ask for the percent, or give the percent and the whole and ask for the part, or give the part and the percent and ask for the value of the whole. The equation for percentages can be rearranged to solve for any of these:

$$percent = \frac{part}{whole}$$

$$part = whole \times percent$$

$$whole = \frac{part}{percent}$$

In the equations above, the percent should always be expressed as a decimal. In order to convert a decimal into a percentage value, simply multiply it by 100. So, if you've read 5 pages (the part) of a 10-page article (the whole), you've read $\frac{5}{10} = 0.5$ or 50%. (The percent sign (%) is used once the decimal has been multiplied by 100.)

Note that when solving these problems, the units for the part and the whole should be the same. If you're reading a book, saying you've read 5 pages out of 15 chapters doesn't make any sense.

Examples

1.   45 is 15% of what number?

Set up the appropriate equation and solve. Don't forget to change 15% to a decimal value:

$$whole = \frac{part}{percent} = \frac{45}{0.15} = \mathbf{300}$$

2.   Jim spent 30% of his paycheck at the fair. He spent $15 for a hat, $30 for a shirt, and $20 playing games. How much was his check? (Round to nearest dollar.)

Set up the appropriate equation and solve:

$$whole = \frac{part}{percent} = \frac{15+30+20}{0.30} = \mathbf{\$217.00}$$

3.   What percent of 65 is 39?

Set up the equation and solve:

$$percent = \frac{part}{whole} = \frac{39}{65} = \mathbf{0.6 \text{ or } 60\%}$$

4.   Greta and Max sell cable subscriptions. In a given month, Greta sells 45 subscriptions and Max sells 51. If 240 total subscriptions were sold in that month, what percent were not sold by Greta or Max?

You can use the information in the question to figure out what percentage of subscriptions were sold by Max and Greta:

$$percent = \frac{part}{whole} = \frac{51+45}{240} = \frac{96}{240} = 0.4 \text{ or } 40\%$$

However, the question asks how many subscriptions weren't sold by Max or Greta. If they sold 40%, then the other salespeople sold 100% − 40% = **60%**.

5.   Grant needs to score 75% on an exam. If the exam has 45 questions, at least how many does he need to answer correctly?

Set up the equation and solve. Remember to convert 75% to a decimal value:

$$part = whole \times percent = 45 \times 0.75 = 33.75,$$ so he needs to answer at least **34 questions correctly**.

Percent Change

PERCENT CHANGE problems will ask you to calculate how much a given quantity changed. The problems are solved in a similar way to regular percent problems, except that instead of using the *part* you'll use the *amount of change*. Note that the sign of the *amount of change* is important: if the original amount has increased the change will be positive, and if it has decreased the change will be negative. Again, in the equations below the percent is a decimal value; you need to multiply by 100 to get the actual percentage.

$$percent\ change = \frac{amount\ of\ change}{original\ amount}$$

$$amount\ of\ change = original\ amount \times percent\ change$$

$$original\ amount = \frac{amount\ of\ change}{percent\ change}$$

Examples

1.   A computer software retailer marks up its games by 40% above the wholesale price when it sells them to customers. Find the price of a game for a customer if the game costs the retailer $25.

Set up the appropriate equation and solve:

amount of change = original amount x *percent change* = 25 × 0.4 = 10

If the amount of change is 10, that means the store adds a markup of $10, so the game costs:

$25 + $10 = **$35**

2.   A golf shop pays its wholesaler $40 for a certain club, and then sells it to a golfer for $75. What is the markup rate?

First, calculate the amount of change:

75 − 40 = 35

Now you can set up the equation and solve. (Note that *markup rate* is another way of saying *percent change*):

$$percent\ change = \frac{amount\ of\ change}{original\ amount} = \frac{35}{40} = 0.875 = \textbf{87.5\%}$$

3.   A store charges a 40% markup on the shoes it sells. How much did the store pay for a pair of shoes purchased by a customer for $63?

You're solving for the original price, but it's going to be tricky because you don't know the amount of change; you only know the new price. To solve, you need to create an expression for the amount of change:

If *original amount = x*

Then *amount of change = 63 − x*

Now you can plug these values into your equation:

$$original\ amount = \frac{amount\ of\ change}{percent\ change}$$

$$x = \frac{63-x}{0.4}$$

The last step is to solve for x:

$0.4x = 63 - x$

$1.4x = 63$

$x = 45$

The store paid **$45 for the shoes**.

4. An item originally priced at $55 is marked 25% off. What is the sale price?

You've been asked to find the sale price, which means you need to solve for the amount of change first:

amount of change = original amount × percent change →
$55 \times 0.25 = 13.75$

Using this amount, you can find the new price. Because it's on sale, we know the item will cost less than the original price:

$55 - 13.75 = 41.25$

The sale price is $41.25.

5. James wants to put in an 18 foot by 51 foot garden in his backyard. If he does, it will reduce the size of this yard by 24%. What will be the area of the remaining yard?

This problem is tricky because you need to figure out what each number in the problem stands for. 24% is obviously the percent change, but what about the measurements in feet? If you multiply these values you get the area of the garden (for more on area see *Area and Perimeter*):

18 ft. × 51 ft. = 918 ft.^{2}

This 918 ft.^{2} is the amount of change—it's how much smaller the lawn is. Now we can set up an equation:

$$original\ amount = \frac{amount\ of\ change}{percent\ change} = \frac{918}{0.24} = 3825$$

If the original lawn was 3825 ft.^{2} and the garden is 918 ft.^{2}, then the remaining area is

$3825 - 918 = 2907$

The remaining lawn covers **2907 ft.^{2}**

Probabilities

A **PROBABILITY** is found by dividing the number of desired outcomes by the number of total possible outcomes. As with percentages, a probability is the ratio of a part to a whole, with the whole being the total number of things that could happen, and the part being the number of those things that would be considered a success. Probabilities can be written using percentages (40%), decimals (0.4), fractions $\left(\frac{2}{5}\right)$, or in words (probability is 2 in 5).

$$probability = \frac{desired\ outcomes}{total\ possible\ outcomes}$$

Examples

1.   A bag holds 3 blue marbles, 5 green marbles, and 7 red marbles. If you pick one marble from the bag, what is the probability it will be blue?

Because there are 15 marbles in the bag (3 + 5 + 7), the total number of possible outcomes is 15. Of those outcomes, 3 would be blue marbles, which is the desired outcome. With that information you can set up an equation:

$$probability = \frac{desired\ outcomes}{total\ possible\ outcomes} = \frac{3}{15} = \frac{1}{5}$$

The probability is **1 in 5 or 0.2 that a blue marble is picked.**

2.   A bag contains 75 balls. If the probability that a ball selected from the bag will be red is 0.6, how many red balls are in the bag?

Because you're solving for desired outcomes (the number of red balls), first you need to rearrange the equation:

$$probability = \frac{desired\ outcomes}{total\ possible\ outcomes} \rightarrow$$

$$desired\ outcomes = probability \times total\ possible\ outcomes$$

In this problem, the desired outcome is choosing a red ball, and the total possible outcomes are represented by the 75 total balls.

$$desired\ outcomes = 0.6 \times 75 = 45$$

There are **45 red balls in the bag.**

3.   A theater has 230 seats: 75 seats are in the orchestra area, 100 seats are in the mezzanine, and 55 seats are in the balcony. If a ticket is selected at random, what is the probability that it will be for either a mezzanine or balcony seat?

In this problem, the desired outcome is a seat in either the mezzanine or balcony area, and the total possible outcomes are represented by the 230 total seats, so the equation should be written as:

$$probability = \frac{desired\ outcomes}{total\ possible\ outcomes} = \frac{100+55}{230} = \mathbf{0.67}$$

4. The probability of selecting a student whose name begins with the letter *s* from a school attendance log is 7%. If there are 42 students whose names begin with *s* enrolled at the school, how many students attend the school?

Because you're solving for total possible outcomes (total number of students), first you need to rearrange the equation:

$$probability = \frac{desired\ outcomes}{total\ possible\ outcomes} \rightarrow$$

$$total\ possible\ outcomes = \frac{desired\ outcomes}{probability}$$

In this problem, you are given a probability (7% or 0.07) and the number of desired outcomes (42). These can be plugged into the equation to solve:

$$total\ possible\ outcomes = \frac{desired\ outcomes}{probability} = \frac{42}{0.07} = \mathbf{600\ students}$$

Algebra
Algebraic Expressions and Equations

Algebraic expressions and equations include a **VARIABLE**, which is a letter standing in for a number. These expressions and equations are made up of **TERMS**, which are groups of numbers and variables (e.g., $2xy$). An **EXPRESSION** is simply a set of terms (e.g., $3x + 2xy$), while an **EQUATION** includes an equal sign (e.g., $3x + 2xy = 17$). When simplifying expressions or solving algebraic equations, you'll need to use many different mathematical properties and operations, including addition, subtraction, multiplication, division, exponents, roots, distribution, and the order of operations.

Evaluating Algebraic Expressions

To evaluate an algebraic expression, simply plug the given value(s) in for the appropriate variable(s) in the expression.

Example

Evaluate $2x + 6y - 3z$ if, $x = 2$, $y = 4$, and $z = -3$.

Plug in each number for the correct variable and simplify:

$2x + 6y - 3z = 2(2) + 6(4) - 3(-3) = 4 + 24 + 9 = 37$

Adding and Subtracting Terms

Only like terms, which have the exact same variable(s), can be added or subtracted. Constants are numbers without variables attached, and those can be added and subtracted together as well. When simplifying an expression, like terms should be added or subtracted so that no individual group of variables occurs in more than one term. For example, the expression $5x + 6xy$ is in its simplest form, while $5x + 6xy - 11xy$ is not because the term *xy* appears more than once.

Example

Simplify the expression $5xy + 7y + 2yz + 11xy - 5yz$.

Start by grouping together like terms:

$(5xy + 11xy) + (2yz - 5yz) + 7y$

Now you can add together each set of like terms:

$16xy + 7y - 3yz$

Multiplying and Dividing Terms

To multiply a single term by another, simply multiply the coefficients and then multiply the variables. Remember that when multiplying variables with exponents, those exponents are added together. For example, $(x^5y)(x^3y^4) = x^8y^5$.

When multiplying a term by a set of terms inside parentheses, you need to **DISTRIBUTE** to each term inside the parentheses as shown below:

When variables occur in both the numerator and denominator of a fraction, they cancel each other out. So, a fraction with variables in its simplest form will not have the same variable on the top and bottom.

Examples

1.   Simplify the expression $(3x^4y^2z)(2y^4z^5)$.

Multiply the coefficients and variables together:

$3 \times 2 = 6$

$y^2 \times y^4 = y^6$

$z \times z^5 = z^6$

Now put all the terms back together:

$6x^4y^6z^6$

2.   Simplify the expression: $(2y^2)(y^3 + 2xy^2z + 4z)$

Multiply each term inside the parentheses by the term $2y^2$:

$(2y^2)(y^3 + 2xy^2z + 4z)$

$(2y^2 \times y^3) + (2y^2 \times 2xy^2z) \times (2y^2 \times 4z)$

$2y^5 + 4xy^4z + 8y^2z$

3.   Simplify the expression: $(5x + 2)(3x + 3)$

Use the acronym FOIL—First, Outer, Inner, Last—to multiply the terms:

First: $5x \times 3x = 15x^2$

Outer: $5x \times 3 = 15x$

Inner: $2 \times 3x = 6x$

Last: $2 \times 3 = 6$

Now combine like terms:

$15x^2 + 21x + 6$

4.   Simplify the expression: $\frac{2x^4 y^3 z}{8x^2 z^3}$

Simplify by looking at each variable and crossing out those that appear in the numerator and denominator:

$$\frac{2}{8} = \frac{1}{4}$$

$$\frac{x^4}{x^2} = \frac{x^2}{1}$$

$$\frac{z}{z^2} = \frac{1}{z}$$

$$\frac{2x^4 y^3 z}{8x^2 z^3} = \frac{x^2 y^3}{4z}$$

Solving Equations

To solve an equation, you need to manipulate the terms on each side to isolate the variable, meaning if you want to find x, you have to get the x alone on one side of the equal sign. To do this, you'll need to use many of the tools discussed above: you might need to distribute, divide, add, or subtract like terms, or find common denominators.

Think of each side of the equation as the two sides of a see-saw. As long as the two people on each end weigh the same amount the see-saw will be balanced: if you have a 120 lb. person on each end, the see-saw is balanced. Giving each of them a 10 lb. rock to hold changes the weight on each end, but the see-saw itself stays balanced. Equations work the same way: you can add, subtract, multiply, or divide whatever you want as long as you do the same thing to both sides.

Most equations you'll see on the TABE can be solved using the same basic steps:

   1.   Distribute to get rid of parentheses.

   2.   Use the least common denominator to get rid of fractions.

   3.   Add/subtract like terms on either side.

   4.   Add/subtract so that constants appear on only one side of the equation.

   5.   Multiply/divide to isolate the variable.

Examples

1. Solve for x: $25x + 12 = 62$

This equation has no parentheses, fractions, or like terms on the same side, so you can start by subtracting 12 from both sides of the equation:

$25x + 12 = 62$

$(25x + 12) - 12 = 62 - 12$

$25x = 50$

Now, divide by 25 to isolate the variable:

$\frac{25x}{25} = \frac{50}{25}$

$x = 2$

2. Solve the following equation for x: $2x - 4(2x + 3) = 24$

Start by distributing to get rid of the parentheses (don't forget to distribute the negative):

$2x - 4(2x + 3) = 24 \rightarrow$

$2x - 8x - 12 = 24$

There are no fractions, so now you can join like terms:

$2x - 8x - 12 = 24 \rightarrow$

$-6x - 12 = 24$

Now add 12 to both sides and divide by -6.

$-6x - 12 = 24$

$(-6x - 12) + 12 = 24 + 12 \rightarrow$

$-6x = 36 \rightarrow$

$\frac{-6x}{-6} = \frac{36}{-6}$

$x = -6$

3. Solve the following equation for x: $\frac{x}{3} + \frac{1}{2} = \frac{x}{6} - \frac{5}{12}$

Start by multiplying by the least common denominator to get rid of the fractions:

$\frac{x}{3} + \frac{1}{2} = \frac{x}{6} - \frac{5}{12} \rightarrow$

$$12\left(\frac{x}{3}+\frac{1}{2}\right) = 12\left(\frac{x}{6}-\frac{5}{12}\right) \rightarrow$$

$$4x + 6 = 2x - 5$$

Now you can isolate x:

$$(4x + 6) - 6 = (2x - 5) - 6 \rightarrow$$

$$4x = 2x - 11 \rightarrow$$

$$(4x) - 2x = (2x - 11) - 2x \rightarrow$$

$$2x = -11 \rightarrow$$

$$x = \frac{11}{2}$$

4. Find the value of x: $2(x + y) - 7x = 14x + 3$

This equation looks more difficult because it has 2 variables, but you can use the same steps to solve for x. First, distribute to get rid of the parentheses and combine like terms:

$$2(x + y) - 7x = 14x + 3 \rightarrow$$

$$2x + 2y - 7x = 14x + 3 \rightarrow$$

$$-5x + 2y = 14x + 3$$

Now you can move the x terms to one side and everything else to the other, and then divide to isolate x:

$$-5x + 2y = 14x + 3 \rightarrow$$

$$-19x = -2y + 3 \rightarrow$$

$$x = \frac{2y-3}{19}$$

Inequalities

INEQUALITIES look like equations, except that instead of having an equal sign, they have one of the following symbols:

> Greater than: The expression left of the symbol is larger than the expression on the right.

< Less than: The expression left of the symbol is smaller than the expression on the right.

≥ Greater than or equal to: The expression left of the symbol is larger than or equal to the expression on the right.

≤ Less than or equal to: The expression left of the symbol is less than or equal to the expression on the right.

Inequalities are solved like linear and algebraic equations. The only difference is that the symbol must be reversed when both sides of the equation are multiplied by a negative number.

Example

Solve for x: $-7x + 2 < 6 - 5x$

Collect like terms on each side as you would for a regular equation:

$-7x + 2 < 6 - 5x \rightarrow$

$-2x < 4$

The direction of the sign switches when you divide by a negative number:

$-2x < 4 \rightarrow$

$x > -2$

Absolute Value

The **ABSOLUTE VALUE** of a number (represented by the symbol $|x|$) is its distance from zero, not its value. For example, $|3| = 3$, and $|-3| = 3$ because both 3 and -3 are three units from zero. The absolute value of a number is always positive.

Equations with absolute values will have two answers, so you need to set up two equations. The first is simply the equation with the absolute value symbol removed. For the second equation, isolate the absolute value on one side of the equation and multiply the other side of the equation by -1.

Examples

1.   Solve for x: $|2x - 3| = x + 1$

Set up the first equation by removing the absolute value symbol, then solve for x:

$|2x - 3| = x + 1$

$2x - 3 = x + 1$

$x = 4$

For the second equation, remove the absolute value and multiply by -1:

$|2x - 3| = x + 1 \rightarrow$

$2x - 3 = -(x + 1) \rightarrow$

$2x - 3 = -x - 1 \rightarrow$

$3x = 2$

$x = 2/3$

Both answers are correct, so the complete answer is $x = 4$ or $\frac{2}{3}$.

2.   Solve for y: $2|y + 4| = 10$

Set up the first equation:

$2(y + 4) = 10 \rightarrow$

$y + 4 = 5 \rightarrow$

$y = 1$

Set up the second equation. Remember to isolate the absolute value before multiplying by -1:

$2|y + 4| = 10 \rightarrow$

$|y + 4| = 5 \rightarrow$

$y + 4 = -5$

$y = -9$

$y = 1$ or -9

Solving Word Problems

Any of the math concepts discussed here can be turned into a word problem, and you'll likely see word problems in various forms throughout the test. (In fact, you may have noticed that several examples in the ratio and proportion sections were word problems.)

The most important step in solving any word problem is to read the entire problem before beginning to solve it: one of the most commonly made mistakes on word problems is providing an answer to a question that wasn't asked. Also, remember that not all of the information given in a problem is always needed to solve it.

When working multiple-choice word problems like those on the TABE, it's important to check your answer. Many of the incorrect choices will be answers that test takers arrive at by making common mistakes. So even if an answer you calculated is given as an answer choice, that doesn't necessarily mean you've worked the problem correctly—you have to check your own work to make sure.

General Steps for Word Problem Solving

Step 1: Read the entire problem and determine what the question is asking for.

Step 2: List all of the given data and define the variables.

Step 3: Determine the formula(s) needed or set up equations from the information in the problem.

Step 4: Solve.

Step 5: Check your answer. (Is the amount too large or small? Are the answers in the correct unit of measure?)

Key Words

Word problems generally contain key words that can help you determine what math processes may be required in order to solve them.

- Addition: added, combined, increased by, in all, total, perimeter, sum, and more than

- Subtraction: how much more, less than, fewer than, exceeds, difference, and decreased

- Multiplication: of, times, area, and product

- Division: distribute, share, average, per, out of, percent, and quotient

- Equals: is, was, are, amounts to, and were

Basic Word Problems

A word problem in algebra is just an equation or a set of equations described using words. Your task when solving these problems is to turn the "story" of the problem into mathematical equations.

Examples

1.   A store owner bought a case of 48 backpacks for $476.00. He sold 17 of the backpacks in his store for $18 each, and the rest were sold to a school for $15 each. What was the salesman's profit?

Start by listing all the data and defining the variable:

total number of backpacks = 48

cost of backpacks = $476.00

backpacks sold in store at price of $18 = 17

backpacks sold to school at a price of $15 = 48 − 17 = 31

total profit = x

Now set up an equation:

total profit = income − cost = (306 + 465) − 476 = 295

The store owner made a profit of **$295**.

2.   Thirty students in Mr. Joyce's room are working on projects over 2 days. The first day, he gave them $\frac{3}{5}$ hour to work. On the second day, he gave them half as much time as the first day. How much time did each student have to work on the project?

Start by listing all the data and defining your variables. Note that the number of students, while given in the problem, is not needed to find the answer:

time on 1st day $= \frac{3}{5}$ hr. = 36 min.

time on 2nd day $= \frac{1}{2}(36) = 18$ min.

total time = x

Now set up the equation and solve:

total time = time on 1st day + time on 2nd day

$x = 36 + 18 = 54$

The students had **54 minutes** to work on the projects.

Distance Word Problems

Distance word problems involve something traveling at a constant or average speed. Whenever you read a problem that involves *how fast*, *how far*, or *for how long*, you should think of the distance equation, $d = rt$, where d stands for distance, r for rate (speed), and t for time.

These problems can be solved by setting up a grid with d, r, and t along the top and each moving object on the left. When setting up the grid, make sure the units are consistent. For example, if the distance is in meters and the time is in seconds, the rate should be meters per second.

Examples

1.   Will drove from his home to the airport at an average speed of 30 mph. He then boarded a helicopter and flew to the hospital with an average speed of 60 mph. The entire distance was 150 miles, and the trip took 3 hours. Find the distance from the airport to the hospital.

The first step is to set up a table and fill in a value for each variable:

DRIVE TIME			
	d	*r*	*t*
driving	d	30	t
flying	$150 - d$	60	$3 - t$

You can now set up equations for driving and flying. The first row gives the equation $d = 30t$, and the second row gives the equation $150 - d = 60(3 - t)$.

Next, you can solve this system of equations. Start by substituting for d in the second equation:

$d = 30t$

$150 - d = 60(3 - t) \rightarrow 150 - 30t = 60(3 - t)$

Now solve for t:

$150 - 30t = 180 - 60t$

$-30 = -30t$

$1 = t$

Although you've solved for t, you're not done yet. Notice that the problem asks for distance. So, you need to solve for d: what the problem asked for. It does not ask for time, but the time is needed to solve the problem.

Driving: $30t = 30$ miles

Flying: $150 - d = 120$ miles

The distance from the airport to the hospital is **120 miles**.

2.   Two cyclists start at the same time from opposite ends of a course that is 45 miles long. One cyclist is riding at 14 mph and the second cyclist is riding at 16 mph. How long after they begin will they meet?

First, set up the table. The variable for time will be the same for each, because they will have been on the road for the same amount of time when they meet:

CYCLIST TIMES			
	d	r	t
Cyclist #1	d	14	t
Cyclist #2	$45 - d$	16	t

Next set up two equations:

Cyclist #1: $d = 14t$

Cyclist #2: $45 - d = 16t$

Now substitute and solve:

$d = 14t$

$45 - d = 16t \rightarrow 45 - 14t = 16t$

$45 = 30t$

$t = 1.5$

They will meet **1.5 hr.** after they begin.

Work Problems
WORK PROBLEMS involve situations where several people or machines are doing work at different rates. Your task is usually to figure out how long it will take these people or machines to complete a task while working

together. The trick to doing work problems is to figure out how much of the project each person or machine completes in the same unit of time. For example, you might calculate how much of a wall a person can paint in 1 hour, or how many boxes an assembly line can pack in 1 minute.

Once you know that, you can set up an equation to solve for the total time. This equation usually has a form similar to the equation for distance, but here *work = rate × time*.

Examples

1.   Bridget can clean an entire house in 12 hours while her brother Tom takes 8 hours. How long would it take for Bridget and Tom to clean 2 houses together?

Start by figuring out how much of a house each sibling can clean on his or her own. Bridget can clean the house in 12 hours, so she can clean $\frac{1}{12}$ of the house in an hour. Using the same logic, Tom can clean $\frac{1}{8}$ of a house in an hour.

By adding these values together, you get the fraction of the house they can clean together in an hour:

$$\frac{1}{12} + \frac{1}{8} = \frac{5}{24}$$

They can do $\frac{5}{24}$ of the job per hour.

Now set up variables and an equation to solve:

t = time spent cleaning (in hours)

h = number of houses cleaned = 2

work = rate × time

$$h = \frac{5}{24}t \rightarrow$$

$$2 = \frac{5}{24}t \rightarrow$$

$$t = \frac{48}{5} = 9\frac{3}{5} \textbf{ hours}$$

2.   Farmer Dan needs to water his cornfield. One hose can water a field 1.25 times faster than a second hose. When both hoses are opened, they water the field in 5 hours. How long would it take to water the field if only the second hose is used?

In this problem you don't know the exact time, but you can still find the hourly rate as a variable:

The first hose completes the job in f hours, so it waters $\frac{1}{f}$ field per hour. The slower hose waters the field in 1.25f, so it waters the field in $\frac{1}{1.25f}$ hours. Together, they take 5 hours to water the field, so they water $\frac{1}{5}$ of the field per hour.

Now you can set up the equations and solve:

$$\frac{1}{f} + \frac{1}{1.25f} = \frac{1}{5} \rightarrow$$

$$1.25f\left(\frac{1}{f}+\frac{1}{1.25f}\right)=1.25f\left(\frac{1}{5}\right)\rightarrow$$

$$1.25+1=0.25f$$

$$2.25=0.25f$$

$$f=9$$

The fast hose takes 9 hours to water the cornfield. The slower hose takes 1.25(9) = **11.25 hours**.

3.   Alex takes 2 hours to shine 500 silver spoons, and Julian takes 3 hours to shine 450 silver spoons. How long will they take, working together, to shine 1000 silver spoons?

Calculate how many spoons each man can shine per hour:

Alex: $\dfrac{500\text{ spoons}}{2\text{ hours}}=\dfrac{250\text{ spoons}}{1\text{ hour}}$

Julian: $\dfrac{450\text{ spoons}}{3\text{ hours}}=\dfrac{150\text{ spoons}}{1\text{ hour}}$

Together: $\dfrac{(250+150)}{1\text{ hour}}=\dfrac{400\text{ spoons}}{1\text{ hour}}$

Now set up an equation to find the time it takes to shine 1000 spoons:

total time $=\dfrac{1\text{ hour}}{400\text{ spoons}}\times 1000\text{ spoons}=\dfrac{1000}{40}\text{hours}=\mathbf{2.5\text{ hours}}$

Statistics and Geometry
Graphs and Charts

These questions require you to interpret information from graphs and charts; they will be pretty straightforward as long as you pay careful attention to detail. There are several different graph and chart types that may appear on the TABE.

Bar Graphs

BAR GRAPHS present the numbers of an item that exist in different categories. The categories are shown on the *x*-axis, and the number of items is shown on the *y*-axis. Bar graphs are usually used to easily compare amounts.

Examples

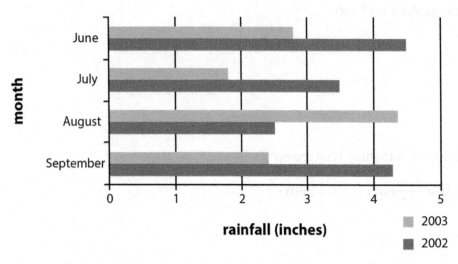

1. The graph above shows rainfall in inches per month. Which month had the least amount of rainfall? Which had the most?

The shortest bar represents the month with the least rain, and the longest bar represents the month with the most rain: **July 2003 had the least**, and **June 2002 had the most**.

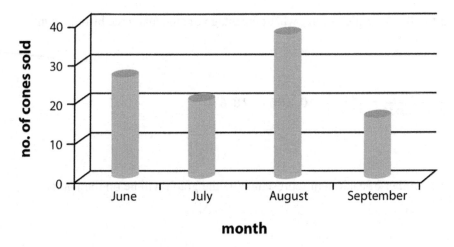

2. Using the graph above, how many more ice cream cones were sold in July than in September?

Tracing from the top of each bar to the scale on the left shows that sales in July were 20 and September sales were 15. So, **5 more cones were sold in July**.

Pie Charts

PIE CHARTS present parts of a whole, and are often used with percentages. Together, all the slices of the pie add up to the total number of items, or 100%.

Examples

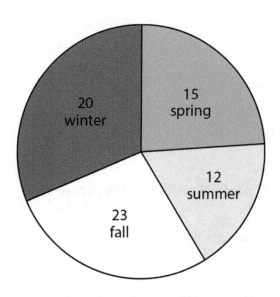

1. The pie chart above shows the distribution of birthdays in a class of students. How many students have birthdays in the spring or summer?

Fifteen students have birthdays in spring and 12 in winter, so there are **27 students** with birthdays in spring or summer.

2.   Using the same Birthday Pie Chart in the example before, what percentage of students have birthdays in winter?

Use the equation for percent:

$$percent = \frac{part}{whole} = \frac{winter\ birthdays}{total\ birthdays} = \frac{20}{20+15+23+12} = \frac{20}{70} = \frac{2}{7} = \mathbf{0.286}\ or\ \mathbf{28.6\%}$$

Line Graphs

LINE GRAPHS show trends over time. The number of each item represented by the graph will be on the *y*-axis, and time will be on the *x*-axis.

Examples

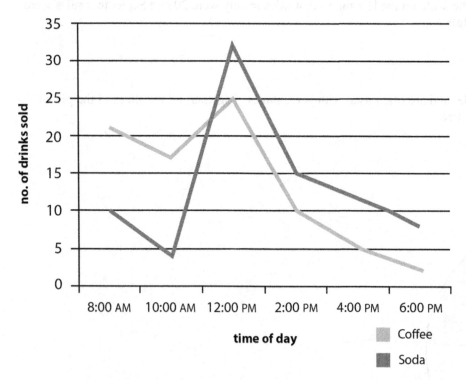

1.   The line graph above shows beverage sales at an airport snack shop throughout the day. Which beverage sold more at 4:00 p.m.?

At 4:00 p.m., approximately 12 sodas and 5 coffees were sold, so more **soda** was sold.

2.   At what time of day were the most beverages sold?

This question is asking for the time of day with the most sales of coffee and soda combined. It is not necessary to add up sales at each time of day to find the answer. Just from looking at the graph, you can see that sales for both beverages were highest at noon, so the answer must be **12:00 p.m.**

Mean, Median, and Mode

MEAN is a math term for average. To find the mean, total all the terms and divide by the number of terms. The MEDIAN is the middle number of a given set. To find the median, put the terms in numerical order; the middle number will be the median. In the case of a set of even numbers, the middle two numbers are averaged. MODE is the number which occurs most frequently within a given set.

Examples

1.   Find the mean of 24, 27, and 18.

Add the terms, then divide by the number of terms:

$$mean = \frac{24+27+18}{3} = 23$$

2.   The mean of three numbers is 45. If two of the numbers are 38 and 43, what is the third number?

Set up the equation for mean with x representing the third number, then solve:

$$mean = \frac{38+43+x}{3} = 45$$

$$38 + 43 + x = 135$$

$$x = 54$$

3.   What is the median of 24, 27, and 18?

Place the terms in order, then pick the middle term:

18, 24, 27

The median is **24**.

4.   What is the median of 24, 27, 18, and 19?

Place the terms in order. Because there are an even number of terms, the median will be the average of the middle 2 terms:

18, 19, 24, 27

$$median = \frac{19+24}{2} = 21.5$$

5.   What is the mode of 2, 5, 4, 4, 3, 2, 8, 9, 2, 7, 2, and 2?

The mode is **2** because it appears the most within the set.

Area and Perimeter

AREA and **PERIMETER** problems will require you to use the equations shown in the table below to find either the area inside a shape or the distance around it (the perimeter). These equations will not be given on the test, so you need to have them memorized on test day.

EQUATIONS		
shape	**area**	**perimeter**
circle	$A = \pi r^2$	$C = 2\pi r = \pi d$
triangle	$A = \frac{b \times h}{2}$	$P = s_1 + s_2 + s_3$
square	$A = s^2$	$P = 4s$
rectangle	$A = l \times w$	$P = 2l + 2w$

Examples

1.   A farmer has purchased 100 m of fencing to put around his rectangular garden. If one side of the garden is 20 m long and the other is 28 m, how much fencing will the farmer have left over?

The perimeter of a rectangle is equal to twice its length plus twice its width:

$P = 2(20) + 2(28) = 96$ m

The farmer has 100 m of fencing, so he'll have
$100 - 96 = $ **4 m left**

2.   Taylor is going to paint a square wall that is 3.5 m tall. What is the total area that Taylor will be painting?

Each side of the square wall is 3.5 m:

$A = 3.5^2 = $ **12.25 m²**

Pythagorean Theorem

Shapes with 3 sides are known as TRIANGLES. In addition to knowing the formulas for their area and perimeter, you should also know the Pythagorean theorem, which describes the relationship between the three sides (a, b, and c) of a right triangle:

$$a^2 + b^2 = c^2$$

Example

Erica is going to run a race in which she'll run 3 miles due north and 4 miles due east. She'll then run back to the starting line. How far will she run during this race?

One leg of her route (the triangle) is missing, but you can find its length using the Pythagorean theorem:

$$a^2 + b^2 = c^2$$

$$3^2 + 4^2 = c^2$$

$$25 = c^2$$

$$c = 5$$

Adding all 3 sides gives the length of the whole race:

$$3 + 4 + 5 = 12 \text{ miles}$$

Pythagorean Theorem

Shapes with 3 sides are known as TRIANGLES. In addition to knowing the formula for their area and perimeter, you should also know the Pythagorean theorem, which describes the relationship between the three sides (a, b, and c) of a right triangle.

Example

Betty is going to run a race in which she'll run 6 miles due south and 8 miles due east. She'll then run back to the starting line. How far will she run during this race?

One of the walls (the triangle) is missing, but you can find its length using the Pythagorean theorem.

$$a^2 + b^2 = c^2$$

$$6^2 + 8^2 = c^2$$

$$100 = c^2$$

Combine all 3 sides to get the length of the whole race.

$$6 + 8 + 10 = 24 \text{ miles}$$

100

Test Your Knowledge: Mathematics

1. Melissa has been thinking about buying a car. She estimates that she would spend $200 per month on car payments, $25 per week on gas, and $600 per year on insurance. About how much would she spend per month? (Note: a month contains four weeks.)

   A) $125

   B) $275

   C) $350

   D) $825

2. Mary works from 5:00 p.m. to 8:30 p.m. on Wednesdays and Thursdays, and from 9:00 a.m. to 3:30 p.m. on Saturdays and Sundays. How many hours does Mary work per week?

   A)   10

   B)   14.5

   C)   18

   D)   20

3. A car rental company charges a daily fee of $48 plus 25% of the daily fee for every hour the car is late. If you rent a car for 2 days and bring it back 2 hours late, what will be the total charge?

   A) $72

   B) $108

   C) $120

   D) $144

4. Rebecca, Emily, and Kate all live on the same straight road. Rebecca lives 1.4 miles from Kate and 0.8 miles from Emily. What is the minimum distance Emily could live from Kate?

   A)   0.6 miles

   B)   0.8 miles

   C)   1.1 miles

   D)   2.2 miles

5. Alex, David, and Rachel go out to dinner. Alex and David decide to split an appetizer that costs $8.50, and Rachel gets her own appetizer that costs $6.50. Rachel also orders lemonade that costs $3. They all order entrées that cost the same price. They split up the bill according to what each person ordered; how much less (before tax and tip) will Alex and David each pay compared to Rachel?

   A) $1.00

   B) $5.00

   C) $5.25

   D) $7.25

6. During a recent storm, it snowed at a rate of 2 centimeters per hour for 190 minutes, 4 centimeters per hour for 40 minutes, 1 centimeter per hour for 280 minutes, and 3 millimeters per hour for 50 minutes. What was the total snowfall to the nearest centimeter?

   A)   10

   B)   13

   C)   14

   D)   16

7. A car dealership is offering a special deal: this year's models are 20% off the list price, and the dealership will pay the first 3 monthly payments. If a car is listed for $26,580, and the monthly payments are $250, how much would a customer save with this deal?

    A) $1,282

    B) $5,566

    C) $6,066

    D) $20,514

8. To get to work, Matt walks 0.75 miles from his house to the bus stop and rides the bus 3.8 miles to his office. If he walks at a pace of 3.6 miles per hour and the bus drives at an average speed of 15 miles per hour, how long is his commute?

    A)   27 minutes, 7 seconds

    B)   27 minutes, 42 seconds

    C)   46 minutes, 16 seconds

    D)   1 hour, 6 minutes, 20 seconds

9. There are 450 students in the 10th grade; of these, 46% are boys. If 21% of the girls have already turned 16, how many girls in the 10th grade are 16?

    A)   10

    B)   47

    C)   51

    D)   94

10. Joe baked brownies in a 9 inch by 11 inch by 2 inch pan. He then cut the brownies into 12 large pieces. Joe ate 2 pieces, his roommate ate 3 pieces, and the dog unfortunately ate half of what was remaining. How many cubic inches of brownies did the dog eat?

    A)   57.75

    B)   82.5

    C)   99

    D)   115.5

11. Which of the following numbers are integers?

I. -7

II. 14.5

III. $\sqrt{64}$

    A)   I only

    B)   II only

    C)   I and III

    D)   II and III

12. Which of the following is an irrational number?

    A)   1.085

    B) $\frac{\pi}{2}$

    C) $\frac{9}{5}$

    D)   16

13. What kind of number is $-\frac{\sqrt{4}}{17}$?

    A)   whole number

    B)   integer

    C)   rational number

    D)   irrational number

14. Simplify the following expression: $\frac{-24(2)^{-1}}{-3}$

    A) -16

    B) -4

    C) $\frac{1}{144}$

    D) 4

15. Simplify the following inequality: $30 - 9x > -6y$

    A) $y < -5 - \frac{2}{3}x$

    B) $y < -5 + \frac{2}{3}x$

    C) $y > -5 + \frac{2}{3}x$

    D) $y > 5 - \frac{2}{3}x$

16. Which of the following is true about negative numbers?

    A)   A negative number raised to a negative number is a positive number.

    B)   A negative number divided by the product of a negative number and a positive number is a positive number.

    C)   The product of a negative number and a positive number, raised to a negative number, is a negative number.

    D)   Both B and C

17. Solve $\frac{\left(\frac{35}{7}\right)^2 - 3^2}{(7+1)}$

    A)   2

    B)   20.7

    C)   60.5

    D)   54,227

18. Solve $(3 + 5)^2 + 24 \div 16 - 5 \div 2$

    A)   0.25

    B)   30.25

    C)   33

    D)   63

19. Which of the following expressions can be simplified to $8x$?

    A) $10 - 2\left(\frac{x^2 - x}{x}\right) + 1$

    B) $\left(\frac{6+9}{7-4}\right)x + 9 - 6x$

    C) $\frac{48}{6 \times 4} + 2^3 x - \frac{4^{(9-6)}}{32}$

    D) $16\left(\frac{x^2}{2^{-1}}\right)$

20. Simplify the following expression: $4 - \frac{1}{2^2} + 24 \div (8 + 12)$

    A)   1.39

    B)   2.74

    C)   4.95

    D)   15.28

21. Which of the following statements about order of operations is false?

   A)   Operations inside parentheses are simplified before operations outside parentheses.

   B)   Multiplication is completed before division.

   C)   Exponents are simplified before addition is completed.

   D)   Addition and subtraction are completed left to right.

22. Simplify: $\sqrt{(375 + 5^3)} - (36 + 64) - 8$

   A)   4.36

   B)   12

   C)   14.98

   D)   28

23. Which of the following expressions is equivalent to the expression $(2 \times x^2) - (y \div 3)^4 + 5 \div 8^2$?

   A) $2(x^2 - y) \div 3^4 + \left(\frac{5}{8}\right)^2$

   B) $(2x)^2 - \frac{y^4 + 5}{3 + 8^2}$

   C) $2x^2 - \left(\frac{y}{3}\right)^4 + \left(\frac{5}{64}\right)$

   D) $\frac{2x^2 - y}{3^4} + \frac{5}{64}$

24. Simplify: $[56 \div (2 \times 2^2)] - 9 \div 3$

   A) -0.667

   B)   4

   C)   34.33

   D)   109

25. Simplify: $3.819 + 14.68 + 0.0006$

   A)   5.2846

   B)   18.4996

   C)   18.505

   D)   52.96

26. Simplify: $59.09 - 5.007 - 6.21$

   A)   47.792

   B)   47.81

   C)   47.873

   D)   47.882

27. How many digits are in the sum $951.4 + 98.908 + 1.053$?

   A)   4

   B)   5

   C)   6

   D)   7

28. Simplify: $105.71 \div 31$

   A)   0.341

   B)   3.41

   C)   34.1

   D)   341

29. Simplify: $54.48 \div 0.6$

   A)   0.908

   B)   9.08

   C)   90.8

   D)   908

104

30. Simplify: 0.08×0.12

    A)   0.0096

    B)   0.096

    C)   0.96

    D)   9.6

31. $\frac{4}{9} \times \frac{1}{2} \times \frac{6}{4} =$

    A) $\frac{2}{9}$

    B) $\frac{1}{3}$

    C) $\frac{2}{3}$

    D) $\frac{64}{3}$

32. $\frac{8}{15}$ is $\frac{1}{6}$ of what number?

    A) $\frac{4}{45}$

    B) $\frac{15}{48}$

    C) $\frac{46}{15}$

    D) $\frac{16}{5}$

33. Simplify the expression: $5\frac{2}{3} \times 1\frac{7}{8} \div \frac{1}{3}$

    A) $3\frac{13}{24}$

    B) $6\frac{3}{4}$

    C) $15\frac{3}{4}$

    D) $31\frac{7}{8}$

34. Ali, Charlotte, and Katie are selling boxes of candy. The shipment of candy arrives at Ali's house; Ali gives $\frac{4}{15}$ of the boxes to Charlotte and $\frac{3}{10}$ of the boxes to Katie. What fraction of the original shipment is left for Ali?

    A) $\frac{3}{10}$

    B) $\frac{8}{15}$

    C) $\frac{13}{30}$

    D) $\frac{17}{30}$

35. Adam is shopping the clearance section at his favorite department store. He finds a jacket that is marked $\frac{1}{3}$ off. His student discount gives him an additional $\frac{1}{5}$ off the original price. By what fraction is the jacket discounted in total?

    A) $\frac{1}{15}$

    B) $\frac{6}{15}$

    C) $\frac{7}{15}$

    D) $\frac{8}{15}$

36. On Monday, Grace fills the gas tank of her car up to $\frac{3}{4}$ full. On Tuesday, she uses $\frac{1}{8}$ of a tank, on Wednesday she uses $\frac{3}{16}$ of a tank, and on Thursday she uses another $\frac{1}{4}$ of a tank. What fraction of the gas tank is full after Thursday?

    A) $\frac{3}{16}$

    B) $\frac{1}{4}$

    C) $\frac{7}{16}$

    D) $\frac{13}{16}$

37. Based on a favorable performance review at work, Matt receives a $\frac{3}{20}$ increase in his hourly wage. If his original hourly wage is represented by w, express his new wage in decimal form.

    A) $0.15w$

    B) $0.85w$

    C) $1.12w$

    D) $1.15w$

38. Express $\frac{15}{25}$ as a decimal.

    A)   0.06

    B)   0.15

    C)   0.375

    D)   0.6

39. How many cents is $\frac{8}{11}$ of a dollar?

    A)   0.72

    B)   0.73

    C)   0.79

    D)   0.81

40. Stephanie eats 0.625 of her pizza. If her pizza was cut into 8 slices, how many slices has she eaten?

    A)   3

    B)   4

    C)   5

    D)   6

41. A carnival game involves picking rubber ducks with numbers written on the bottom. There is a 0.05 probability of picking a rubber duck with the number 3. What fraction of the rubber ducks are numbered 3?

    A) $\frac{1}{20}$

    B) $\frac{3}{20}$

    C) $\frac{1}{5}$

    D) $\frac{1}{15}$

42. A chocolate chip cookie recipe calls for 2.375 cups of flour. Express this quantity as a fraction.

    A) $2\frac{3}{5}$ cups

    B) $2\frac{3}{8}$ cups

    C) $2\frac{2}{8}$ cups

    D) $2\frac{1}{3}$ cups

43. A marinade recipe calls for 2 tablespoons of lemon juice for $\frac{1}{4}$ cup of olive oil. How much lemon juice should you use with $\frac{2}{3}$ cup olive oil?

    A) $5\frac{1}{3}$ tablespoons

    B) $\frac{3}{4}$ tablespoons

    C)   4 tablespoons

    D) $2\frac{1}{3}$ tablespoons

44. A material's specific heat capacity is the amount of energy needed to increase the temperature of 1 gram of that material by 1 degree Celsius. If the specific heat capacity of aluminum is $0.900 \frac{J}{g \cdot °C}$, how many joules of energy does it take to increase the temperature of 2 grams of aluminum by 4 degrees Celsius?

    A)   3.6 joules

    B)   0.1 joules

    C)   7.2 joules

    D)   5.6 joules

45. The density of cork is approximately 0.24 grams per cubic centimeter. How much water would 100 grams of cork displace?

    A) 3.67 cm^3

    B) 1.24 cm^3

    C) 24 cm^3

    D) 4.17 cm^3

46. Stephanie's car uses an average of 29 miles per gallon. $\frac{1}{3}$ of her gas tank holds 3.5 gallons. How many miles can she drive on a full tank of gas?

    A)   33.8 miles

    B)   101.5 miles

    C)   367.5 miles

    D)   304.5 miles

47. Adam owns 4 times as many shirts as he has pairs of pants, and he has 5 pairs of pants for every 2 pairs of shoes. What is the ratio of Adam's shirts to Adam's shoes?

    A)   25 shirts : 1 pair shoes

    B)   10 shirts : 1 pair shoes

    C)   20 shirts : 1 pair shoes

    D)   15 shirts : 2 pairs shoes

48. A box of instant rice provides the following instructions: "For 4 servings, stir 2 cups of rice into 1.75 cups of boiling water." How many cups of water are needed for 6 servings of rice?

    A)   2.625 cups

    B)   13.7 cups

    C)   3 cups

    D)   1.167 cups

49. A restaurant employs servers, hosts, and managers in a ratio of 9:2:1. If there are 36 total employees, how many hosts are there?

    A)   4

    B)   3

    C)   6

    D)   8

50. 7 is what percent of 60?

    A)   11.67%

    B)   4.20%

    C)   8.57%

    D)   10.11%

51. What percent of 14 is 35?

    A)   4.9%

    B)   2.5%

    C)   40%

    D)   250%

52. 15 is 8 percent of what number?

    A)   1.2

    B)   53.3

    C)   187.5

    D)   120

53. On a given day at the local airport, 15 flights were delayed and 62 left on time. What percentage of the flights was delayed?

    A)   24.2%

    B)   19.5%

    C)   80.5%

    D)   22.4%

54. Gym A offers a monthly membership for 80% of the cost at Gym B; the cost at Gym B is 115% the cost at Gym C. What percentage of the cost at Gym C does Gym A charge?

    A)   35%

    B)   97%

    C)   70%

    D)   92%

55. If there are 380 female students in a graduating class, and male students represent 60% of the graduating class, how many total students are there in the class?

    A)   633

    B)   950

    C)   570

    D)   720

56. What is 18% of 76% of 15,000?

    A)   3,553

    B)   2,052

    C)   633

    D)   8,700

57. A manufacturer sells a product to a retailer for 350% of the production cost. The retailer sells the product to consumers for 600% of the production cost. What percentage of her purchase cost is the retailer's profit when she sells to consumers?

    A)   250%

    B)   41.7%

    C)   58.3%

    D)   71.4%

58. Evaluate the expression $\frac{4x}{x-1}$ when $x = 5$.

    A)   3

    B)   4

    C)   5

    D)   6

59. Evaluate the expression $\frac{x^2-2y}{y}$ when $x = 20$ and $y = \frac{x}{2}$.

    A)   0

    B)   38

    C)   36

    D)   19

60. Evaluate the expression $\sqrt{(x^{-1})4x}$ when $x = y + 3$ and $y = 14$.

    A)   2

    B) -2

    C)   34

    D) $\frac{1}{\sqrt{2}}$

61. Simplify: $3x^3 + 4x - (2x + 5y) + y$

    A) $3x^3 + 2x + y$

    B) $11x - 4y$

    C) $3x^3 + 2x - 4y$

    D) $29x - 4y$

62. Find the sum: $2\left(\frac{y}{x}\right) + \frac{1}{x}(3y)$

    A) $\frac{y}{x}$

    B) $\frac{5y}{x^2}$

    C) $\frac{5y}{6x}$

    D) $\frac{5y}{x}$

63. Simplify the expression: $x^3 - 3x^2 + (2x)^3 - x$

    A) $x^3 - 3x^2 + 7x$

    B) $9x^3 - 3x^2 - x$

    C) $20x$

    D) $7x^3 - 3x^2 - x$

64. What is the range of the function $f(x) = x^2 + 2$?

    A)   all real numbers

    B)   all real numbers greater than 2

    C)   all real numbers greater than or equal to 2

    D)   all real numbers less than or equal to 2

65. Consider the function $f(x) = -2x - 5$ with the range $\{17, 15, 11, -5\}$. Define the domain.

    A)   domain $= \{-11, -10, -8, 0\}$

    B)   domain $= \{-39, -35, -27, 5\}$

    C)   domain $= \{-14, -11, -6, 0\}$

    D)   domain $= \{-6, -5, -3, 5\}$

66. Which of the following is always true of functions?

    A)   For each value in the range, there is only one value in the domain.

    B)   For each value in the domain, there is only one value in the range.

    C)   The range of a function includes all real numbers.

    D)   The domain of a function includes all real numbers.

67. If $f(x) = 3^x - 2$, evaluate $f(5)$.

    A)   27

    B)   243

    C)   241

    D)   13

68. Which of the following is true of the function $f(x) = 8^x$?

    A)   The graph of the function has a horizontal asymptote along the negative x-axis.

    B)   The graph of the function has a horizontal asymptote along the positive x-axis.

    C)   The graph of the function has a vertical asymptote along the negative y-axis.

    D)   The graph of the function has a vertical asymptote along the positive y-axis.

69. If $f(x) = 0.5^x + 1$, evaluate $f(-2)$.

    A)   0.75

    B)   2

    C)   4

    D)   5

70. If $f(x) = e^{2x}$, evaluate $\ln[f(3)]$.

    A)   3

    B)   5

    C)   6

    D) $\frac{1}{e^6}$

71. Which of the following is true of the function $f(x) = 1^x - 3$?

    A)   The graph of the function is a horizontal line at $y = -2$.

    B)   The graph of the function is a vertical line at $x = -2$.

    C)   The graph of the function has a horizontal asymptote at $y = -3$.

    D)   The graph of the function has a vertical asymptote at $x = -3$.

72. A 650 square foot apartment in Boston costs $1800 per month to rent. What is the monthly rent per square foot?

    A) $13

    B) $0.36

    C) $2.77

    D) $3.66

73. A radio station plays songs that last an average of 3.5 minutes and has commercial breaks that last 2 minutes. If the station is required to play 1 commercial break for every 4 songs, how many songs can the station play in an hour?

    A)   15

    B)   11

    C)   16

    D)   17

74. Students in a particular math class received an average score of 84% on a recent test. If there are 20 boys and 30 girls in the class, and the boys' average score was 82%, what was the girls' average score?

   A)   83%

   B)   88%

   C)   85%

   D)   86%

75. $\frac{1}{10}$ of a company's employees are in their 20s, $\frac{2}{5}$ are in their 30s, $\frac{1}{3}$ are in their 40s and the remaining 5 employees are 50 or older. How many employees work at the company?

   A)   5

   B)   30

   C)   60

   D)   24

76. A chemical experiment requires that a solute be diluted with 4 parts (by mass) water for every 1 part (by mass) solute. If the desired mass for the solution is 90 grams, how much solute should be used?

   A)   15 grams

   B)   72 grams

   C)   22.5 grams

   D)   18 grams

77. Lisa rides her bike at 10 miles per hour for 28 minutes, 15 miles per hour for 49 minutes, and 12 miles per hour for 15 minutes. How far did she travel in total?

   A)   11.95 miles

   B)   18.91 miles

   C)   19.92 miles

   D)   20.21 miles

78. A plane makes a trip of 246 miles. For some amount of time, the plane's speed is 115 miles per hour. For the remainder of the trip, the plane's speed is 250 miles per hour. If the total trip time is 72 minutes, how long did the plane fly at 115 miles per hour?

   A)   18 minutes

   B)   23 minutes

   C)   24 minutes

   D)   34 minutes

79. A runner completes a 12 mile race in 1 hour and 30 minutes. If her pace for the first part of the race was 7 minutes per mile, and her pace for the second part of the race was 8 minutes per mile, for how many miles did she sustain her pace of 7 minutes per mile?

   A)   4 miles

   B)   5.5 miles

   C)   6 miles

   D)   7 miles

80. A swimmer is swimming 25 meter sprints. If he swims 4 sprints in 3 minutes, 6 more sprints in 5 minutes, and then 4 final sprints in 2 minutes, what was his average speed during his sprints?

A)   35 meters per minute

B)   1.4 meters per minute

C)   350 meters per minute

D)   17.9 meters per minute

81. A cheetah in the wild can accelerate from 0 miles per hour to 60 miles per hour in 2.8 seconds. Then, it can sustain a speed of 60 miles per hour for up to 60 seconds before it has to rest. How much total distance can the cheetah travel from when it starts to accelerate to the moment it has to stop?

A)   3,684 miles

B)   2.4 miles

C)   1.046 miles

D)   1.023 miles

82. 2 warehouse workers can pack 5 boxes in 6 minutes. If 1 worker can pack 6 boxes by himself in 15 minutes, how many boxes can the other worker pack by himself in the same amount of time?

A)   6.5 boxes

B)   6 boxes

C)   12.5 boxes

D)   7.5 boxes

83. John and Jake are working at a car wash. It takes John 1 hour to wash 3 cars; Jake can wash 3 cars in 45 minutes. If they work together, how many cars can they wash in 1 hour?

A)   6 cars

B)   7 cars

C)   9 cars

D)   12 cars

84. Ed is going to fill his swimming pool with a garden hose. His neighbor, a volunteer firefighter, wants to use a fire hose attached to the hydrant in the front yard to make the job go faster. The fire hose sprays 13.5 times as much water per minute as the garden hose. If the garden hose and the fire hose together can fill the pool in 107 minutes, how long would it have taken to fill the pool with the garden hose alone?

A)   7 hours, 37.9 min

B)   7 hours, 55.6 min

C)   1 day, 4.5 min

D)   1 day, 1 hour, 51.5 min

85. Suppose Mark can mow the entire lawn in 47 minutes, and Mark's dad can mow the entire lawn in 53 minutes. If Mark and his dad work together (each with their own lawnmowers), how long will it take them to mow the entire lawn?

A)   15.6 minutes

B)   24.9 minutes

C)   26.5 minutes

D)   50 minutes

86. Rafael and Marco are repainting their garage. If Rafael can paint 1/6 of the garage in 20 minutes, and Marco can paint 1/5 of the garage in 30 minutes, how long will it take them to paint the entire garage if they work together?

A)   1 hr, 6.7 min

B)   2 hr, 43.6 min

C)   0 hr, 54 min

D)   6 hr, 12 min

87. Find the area of a rectangular athletic field that is 100 meters long and 45 meters wide.

A)   290 meters

B)   4,500 m^2

C)   145 m^2

D)   4.5 km^2

88. Melissa is ordering fencing to enclose a square area of 5625 square feet. How many feet of fencing does she need?

A)   75 feet

B)   150 feet

C)   300 feet

D)   5,625 feet

89. Adam is painting a 4-walled shed. The shed is 5 feet wide, 4 feet deep, and 7 feet high. How much paint will Adam need?

A)   126 ft^2

B)   140 ft^3

C)   63 ft^2

D)   46 feet

90. James is building an octagonal gazebo with equal sides in his backyard. If one side is 5.5 feet wide, what is the perimeter of the entire gazebo?

A)   22 feet

B)   30.25 feet

C)   44 feet

D)   242 feet

91. A courtyard garden has flower beds in the shape of 4 equilateral triangles arranged so that their bases enclose a square space in the middle for a fountain. If the space for the fountain has an area of 1 square meter, find the total area of the flower beds and fountain space.

A)   1.73 m^2

B)   2.73 m^2

C)   1.43 m^2

D)   3 m^2

92. 2 identical circles are drawn next to each other with their sides just touching; both circles are enclosed in a rectangle whose sides are tangent to the circles. If each circle's radius is 2 inches, find the area of the rectangle.

A)   24 cm^2

B)   8 cm^2

C)   32 cm^2

D)   16 cm^2

93. A grain silo is cylinder-shaped with a height of 10 meters and a diameter of 3.2 meters. What is the surface area of the silo, including the top but not the base?

   A)   233.23 m^2

   B)   265.40 m^2

   C)   116.61 m^2

   D)   108.57 m^2

94. Find the total surface area of a box that is 12 inches long, 18 inches wide, and 6 inches high.

   A)   144 in^2

   B)   1,296 in^3

   C)   792 in^2

   D)   396 in^2

95. A developer is designing a rectangular parking lot for a new shopping center. A 20-foot-wide driving lane circles the interior, which has 6 rows of parking spaces divided by 5 driving lanes. Each row of parking spaces is 36 feet wide and 90 feet long. The driving lanes are 20 feet wide and 90 feet long. What is the perimeter of the entire parking lot?

   A)   972 feet

   B)   486 feet

   C)   812 feet

   D)   852 feet

96. A cylindrical canister is 9 inches high and has a diameter of 5 inches. What is the maximum volume this canister can hold?

   A)   176.7 in^2

   B)   45 in^2

   C)   141.4 in^2

   D)   706.9 in^2

97. If a spherical water balloon is filled with 113 milliliters of water, what is the approximate radius of the balloon?

   A)   4.0 centimeters

   B)   3.0 centimeters

   C)   3.6 centimeters

   D)   3.3 centimeters

98. A circular swimming pool has a circumference of 49 feet. What is the diameter of the pool?

   A)   15.6 feet

   B)   12.3 feet

   C)   7.8 feet

   D)   17.8 feet

99. A pizza has a diameter of 10 inches. If you cut a slice with a central angle of 40 degrees, how many inches of crust does that slice include?

   A)   31.4 inches

   B)   7.0 inches

   C)   3.5 inches

   D)   3.3 inches

100. A pizza has a diameter of 10 inches. If you cut a slice with a central angle of 40 degrees, what will be the surface area of the pizza slice?

   A) 9.2 in^2

   B) 8.7 in^2

   C) 3.5 in^2

   D) 17.4 in^2

101. Liz is installing a tile backsplash. If each tile is an equilateral triangle with sides that measure 6 centimeters in length, how many tiles does she need to cover an area of 1800 square centimeters?

   A)   36 tiles

   B)   100 tiles

   C)   50 tiles

   D)   300 tiles

102. The perimeter of an isosceles triangle is 25 centimeters. If the legs are twice as long as the base, what is the length of the base?

   A)   5 centimeters

   B)   10 centimeters

   C)   15 centimeters

   D)   8.3 centimeters

103. The table below shows the number of hours worked by employees during the week. What is the median number of hours worked per week by the employees?

Employee	Suzanne	Joe	Mark	Ellen	Jill	Rob	Nicole	Deb
Hours worked per week	42	38	25	50	45	46	17	41

   A)   38

   B)   41

   C)   42

   D)   41.5

104. The table below shows the number of hours worked by employees during the week. What is the difference between the median and mean number of hours worked per week?

Employee	Suzanne	Joe	Mark	Ellen	Jill	Rob	Nicole	Deb
Hours worked per week	42	38	25	50	45	46	17	41

   A)   38

   B)   3.5

   C)   1.5

   D)   41.5

105. Meg rolled a 6-sided die 4 times, and her first 3 rolls were 1, 3, and 5. If the average of the 4 rolls is 2.5, what was the result of her fourth roll?

    A) 1

    B) 2

    C) 3

    D) 5

106. The data set below shows number of instruments played by students in the 7th and 10th grades. What is the difference in the average number of instruments played by 7th- and 10th-graders?

Student	Alison	Dana	Jerry	Sam	Luke	Philip	Briana	Laura	Angie
Grade	7	10	7	7	10	7	10	10	7
# Instruments played	2	0	1	1	1	2	1	0	2

    A) 2.1

    B) 1

    C) 0.9

    D) 0.5

107. Which of the following is a measure of central tendency that is most affected by an outlier in the data set?

    A) mean

    B) median

    C) mode

    D) range

108. Which of the following measures of central tendency changes when a constant is added to every data point in a data set?

    A) mean

    B) median

    C) mode

    D) all of the above

109. A data set contains n points with a mean of μ. If a new data point with the value x is included in the data set, which of the following expressions is equal to the new mean?

    A) $\dfrac{\mu+x}{n}$

    B) $\dfrac{\mu n+x}{n+1}$

    C) $\dfrac{\mu n+x}{n}$

    D) $\dfrac{(\mu+x)n}{n+1}$

116

110. The average height of female students in a class is 64.5 inches, and the average height of male students in the class is 69 inches. If there are 1.5 times as many female students as male students, what is the average height for the entire class?

A) 67.2 inches

B) 66.75 inches

C) 67.5 inches

D) 66.3 inches

111. What is the probability of selecting a queen of hearts or a queen of diamonds from a normal deck of 52 playing cards?

A) $\frac{1}{2704}$

B) $\frac{1}{104}$

C) $\frac{1}{26}$

D) $\frac{1}{52}$

112. There are 3 red, 4 blue, and 6 black marbles in a bag. When Carlos reaches into the bag and selects a marble without looking, what are the chances that he will select a black marble?

A) 0.46

B) 0.86

C) 0.31

D) 0.23

Mathematics Answer Key

1. C	39. B	77. C
2. D	40. C	78. C
3. C	41. A	79. C
4. A	42. B	80. A
5. C	43. A	81. D
6. C	44. C	82. A
7. C	45. D	83. B
8. B	46. D	84. D
9. C	47. B	85. B
10. A	48. A	86. A
11. D	49. C	87. B
12. B	50. A	88. C
13. D	51. D	89. A
14. D	52. C	90. C
15. C	53. B	91. B
16. D	54. D	92. C
17. A	55. B	93. D
18. D	56. B	94. C
19. C	57. D	95. A
20. C	58. C	96. A
21. B	59. B	97. B
22. B	60. A	98. A
23. C	61. C	99. C
24. B	62. D	100. B
25. B	63. B	101. B
26. C	64. C	102. A
27. D	65. A	103. D
28. B	66. B	104. B
29. C	67. C	105. A
30. A	68. A	106. C
31. B	69. D	107. A
32. D	70. C	108. D
33. D	71. A	109. B
34. C	72. C	110. D
35. D	73. A	111. C
36. A	74. C	112. A
37. D	75. B	
38. D	76. D	

Exclusive Trivium Test Tips

Here at Trivium Test Prep, we strive to offer you the exemplary test tools that help you pass your exam the first time. This book includes an overview of important concepts, example questions throughout the text, and practice test questions. But we know that learning how to successfully take a test can be just as important as learning the content being tested. In addition to excelling on the TABE, we want to give you the solutions you need to be successful every time you take a test. Our study strategies, preparation pointers, and test tips will help you succeed as you take the TABE and any test in the future!

Study Strategies

1. Spread out your studying. By taking the time to study a little bit every day, you strengthen your understanding of the testing material, so it's easier to recall that information on the day of the test. Our study guides make this easy by breaking up the concepts into sections with example practice questions, so you can test your knowledge as you read.

2. Create a study calendar. The sections of our book make it easy to review and practice with example questions on a schedule. Decide to read a specific number of pages or complete a number of practice questions every day. Breaking up all of the information in this way can make studying less overwhelming and more manageable.

3. Set measurable goals and motivational rewards. Follow your study calendar and reward yourself for completing reading, example questions, and practice problems and tests. You could take yourself out after a productive week of studying or watch a favorite show after reading a chapter. Treating yourself to rewards is a great way to stay motivated.

4. Use your current knowledge to understand new, unfamiliar concepts. When you learn something new, think about how it relates to something you know really well. Making connections between new ideas and your existing understanding can simplify the learning process and make the new information easier to remember.

5. Make learning interesting! If one aspect of a topic is interesting to you, it can make an entire concept easier to remember. Stay engaged and think about how concepts covered on the exam can affect the things you're interested in. The sidebars throughout the text offer additional information that could make ideas easier to recall.

6. Find a study environment that works for you. For some people, absolute silence in a library results in the most effective study session, while others need the background noise of a coffee shop to fuel productive studying. There are many websites that generate white noise and recreate the sounds of different environments for studying. Figure out what distracts you and what engages you and plan accordingly.

7. Take practice tests in an environment that reflects the exam setting. While it's important to be as comfortable as possible when you study, practicing taking the test exactly as you'll take it on test day will make you more prepared for the actual exam. If your test starts on a Saturday morning, take your practice test on a Saturday morning. If you have access, try to find an empty classroom that has desks like the desks at testing center. The more closely you can mimic the testing center, the more prepared you'll feel on test day.

8. Study hard for the test in the days before the exam, but take it easy the night before and do something relaxing rather than studying and cramming. This will help decrease anxiety, allow you to get a better

night's sleep, and be more mentally fresh during the big exam. Watch a light-hearted movie, read a favorite book, or take a walk, for example.

Preparation Pointers

1. Preparation is key! Don't wait until the day of your exam to gather your pencils, calculator, identification materials, or admission tickets. Check the requirements of the exam as soon as possible. Some tests require materials that may take more time to obtain, such as a passport-style photo, so be sure that you have plenty of time to collect everything. The night before the exam, lay out everything you'll need, so it's all ready to go on test day! We recommend at least two forms of ID, your admission ticket or confirmation, pencils, a high protein, compact snack, bottled water, and any necessary medications. Some testing centers will require you to put all of your supplies in a clear plastic bag. If you're prepared, you will be less stressed the morning of, and less likely to forget anything important.
2. If you're taking a pencil-and-paper exam, test your erasers on paper. Some erasers leave big, dark stains on paper instead of rubbing out pencil marks. Make sure your erasers work for you and the pencils you plan to use.
3. Make sure you give yourself your usual amount of sleep, preferably at least 7 – 8 hours. You may find you need even more sleep. Pay attention to how much you sleep in the days before the exam, and how many hours it takes for you to feel refreshed. This will allow you to be as sharp as possible during the test and make fewer simple mistakes.
4. Make sure to make transportation arrangements ahead of time, and have a backup plan in case your ride falls through. You don't want to be stressing about how you're going to get to the testing center the morning of the exam.
5. Many testing locations keep their air conditioners on high. You want to remember to bring a sweater or jacket in case the test center is too cold, as you never know how hot or cold the testing location could be. Remember, while you can always adjust for heat by removing layers, if you're cold, you're cold.

Test Tips

1. Go with your gut when choosing an answer. Statistically, the answer that comes to mind first is often the right one. This is assuming you studied the material, of course, which we hope you have done if you've read through one of our books!
2. For true or false questions: if you genuinely don't know the answer, mark it true. In most tests, there are typically more true answers than false answers.
3. For multiple-choice questions, read ALL the answer choices before marking an answer, even if you think you know the answer when you come across it. You may find your original "right" answer isn't necessarily the best option.
4. Look for key words: in multiple choice exams, particularly those that require you to read through a text, the questions typically contain key words. These key words can help the test taker choose the correct answer or confuse you if you don't recognize them. Common keywords are: *most, during, after, initially,* and *first.* Be sure you identify them before you read the available answers. Identifying the key words makes a huge difference in your chances of passing the test.
5. Narrow answers down by using the process of elimination: after you understand the question, read each answer. If you don't know the answer right away, use the process of elimination to narrow down the answer choices. It is easy to identify at least one answer that isn't correct. Continue to narrow down the

choices before choosing the answer you believe best fits the question. By following this process, you increase your chances of selecting the correct answer.

6. Don't worry if others finish before or after you. Go at your own pace, and focus on the test in front of you.

7. Relax. With our help, we know you'll be ready to conquer the TABE. You've studied and worked hard!

Keep in mind that every individual takes tests differently, so strategies that might work for you may not work for someone else. You know yourself best and are the best person to determine which of these tips and strategies will benefit your studying and test taking. Best of luck as you study, test, and work toward your future!

DATE DUE

JUN 2 0 2017
OCT 2 2 2019
MAR 0 3 2020

PRINTED IN U.S.A.

CPSIA information can be obtained
at www.ICGtesting.com
Printed in the USA
LVOW05s1602280317
528763LV00008B/293/P

9 781635 300895